# Trails through the Jungle

## Life Stories from South Sumatra

### Hildegard Berg

VTR

Publications

ISBN 978-3-941750-04-3

© 2013
VTR Publications
Gogolstr. 33, 90475 Nürnberg, Germany
http://www.vtr-online.com

Translated from the original German title
*Leben wo der Pfeffer wächst: Erinnerungen aus Südsumatra,*
published by OM Books, Passaustr. 19, 4030 Linz, Austria

Copyright German edition by WEC International Germany, 2009

Translation: Ulrike Hunt / Daphne Spragett

Cover image: Jörg Ehlerding
Images: Hildegard Berg
Layout: VTR Publications

Printed by Lightning Source

# Contents

# Maps

INDONESIA

SOUTH SUMATRA

Introduction

# How the Gospel Came to the Serawai People

Early in the 1960s communist activities were taking place all over Indonesia, even in the remote villages of Sumatra. Pak Muin, a Serawai man
from Siginim, a village on the west coast of southern Sumatra, had received
an invitation to a seminar in Palembang, the city on the island's east coast.
He was keen to attend and be trained as a communist leader. The people of
his village hoped that through this doctrine they would all receive a new
perspective on life.

Pak Muin was ill when he arrived in Palembang and was admitted to the
Methodist clinic for treatment. There he heard the Gospel for the first time.
Later, at the communist seminar, he heard Marx's philosophies – that religion is the opium of the people and that there is no God. For him the matter
was clear, "We are Muslims," he said, "and we know that there is a God.
We pray to him daily. If that is what communism is about, then it is not for
us!" Disappointed, he left the meeting in Palembang.

On his way home Pak Muin travelled through the sleepy fishing town of
Bengkulu on the west coast of Sumatra. As he wandered alone through the
streets, a car with the word "Injil", the Indonesian word for "Gospel", written on it, grabbed his attention. Wasn't that what he had heard about at the
clinic? He followed the car to a small Batak[1] church.

On that particular afternoon they were celebrating Christmas. Pak Muin
was gripped by the message that God had come to live among men because
he loves them and wants to give them the gift of a meaningful life. He
gladly took all the scripture tracts offered to him. That was Christmas 1963.

A few days later Pak Muin arrived back at his village. In the evening the
men of the village met at his home, curious to hear what he had discovered
on his travels. They sat on mats in the large room of Pak Muin's traditional
wooden house and listened as he related his adventures. He told them that
the communists claim that there is no God. He told them too about the
Christian message he had heard of the love of God towards man. Together

---

[1]  The *Batak* are a people group in northern Sumatra, amongst whom Christian Missionaries, also from Germany (e.g. Ludwig Nommensen), have been working since
1861. Today there is a large number of Christian believers there.

they read the scripture tracts he had been given. They talked about this message, but there was a lot they did not really understand. Then somebody had an idea, "Why don't we write a letter to the Christians and invite them to explain about the God of love to us in a bit more detail?"

Together they wrote a letter and addressed it to "The Injil in Bengkulu". As the car displaying the word "Injil" was well known in the town, it was not difficult for the postman, who was himself a Christian, to deliver the letter to the correct address.

The car belonged to Mr. Harrington, a missionary from New Zealand. He was delighted to receive the invitation to explain the good news in the villages to the south of Bengkulu. He and his co-workers had been praying for a long time for the Serawai people and for an opening among them to preach the gospel! He sent the evangelist Pak Tobing to them. Pak Tobing was a Batak man who had worked in the Serawai area as a teacher and was familiar with their language and customs. His wife was a Serawai girl who prayed daily for her people.

Night after night and into the early hours of the morning, Pak Tobing sat with the men of the villages of Siginim, drinking coffee and talking with them about the gospel. He was even asked to preach about the good news in the mosques! After his first visit to this area about 200 people professed faith and became Christians.

Mr. Harrington approached the Bible school in Batu, East Java, for help and asked for student trainees to come over to South Sumatra. Their role would be to affirm and disciple the young Christians in their faith. A team, led by Pak Oktavianus, spent three months in the area. Around 300 people, former Muslims, asked to be baptised. Some of the students, including Pak Acis and Pak Wagiono, decided to stay on for an extra year to continue to disciple the new believers. And so, over the following months, a small congregation sprang up.

In October 1965 the communists in Indonesia attempted a coup which, however, failed. Two years later a man died in Napal Melintang. As the deceased was an active communist, the local Imam[2] refused to bury him. The people there had heard of the "good shepherd" of Siginim so the family sent two young men over to fetch the evangelist. They trekked through the jungle for nine hours and finally arrived back at Napal Melingtang with the evangelist. By that time the deceased had been buried, but the evangelist found the people ready to hear the gospel. And so a Christian congregation sprung up in that village as well.

---

[2] An *Imam* is a Muslim spiritual leader.

There, as in Siginim, the children of the Christians were soon disadvantaged in the state schools. So the Christian communities founded and built their own Christian schools. Christian teachers came from West Timor, where there was a revival at the time.

In 1974 the Serawai congregations joined together to form Gereja Kristen Injili Sumatera Selatan (GEKISUS) – the Evangelical Christian Churches of Southern Sumatra.

Part 1

# Preparation

# Chapter 1

# The Challenge

In my hands I held a letter from the Wycliffe Bible Translators, presumably an answer to my enquiry.

It was 1976. I had completed my dissertation, had two more oral exams to go and then I would be finished with my IT studies. It was time to think about my next steps. Not that I hadn't already done so! But I was not simply looking for a job. I was trying to work out how I could use what I had learnt for God. Would it be in a career in Germany or, perhaps, in missions? Where did God want me to be and for what was I suited?

While I was working on my dissertation, a friend from the SMD (the student mission in Germany) who was a graduate of the University of Karlsruhe had mentioned Wycliffe Bible Translators[3] to me. He had told me that this mission agency was already using computers for their work of Bible translation. At a meeting a few months later the speaker said, "God can use any occupation in His service. Tell me what you are studying and I will tell you where that could be used to serve Him." He also pointed me in the direction of Wycliffe. So I had sent an enquiry to the German Headquarters of the Wycliffe Bible Translators.

Apprehensive, I read the answer. At that time they were not using computers in their work in Germany and therefore did not need any IT specialists. I began to feel relieved. But the letter continued to say that they had mathematicians and IT specialists working in their ranks as Bible translators and that they tended to be skilled at language analysis. Finally there was the challenge to pray and to consider whether this could be God's way for me.

"Me and language work," I thought. "What a laugh! God knows I am not at all gifted in languages! I nearly failed my final English exam, and German has always been a battle for me. Okay, my Latin and grammar were fine and I'd have no problem with analytical thinking, but..."

I was put off by the idea of translation work and tried to ignore it. And yet I couldn't simply dismiss it. After all, it said in the letter that I should pray about it. "Okay," I decided, "I will prove to God that I am not cut out for this

---

[3] *Wycliffe Bible Translators* is a mission agency whose main aim is to translate the Bible into indigenous languages.

work!" I figured the best way of proving the absurdity of it all would come from launching myself fully into this undertaking. So I asked Wycliffe for more information about their translation work. "If I have a better understanding about the work, it will be easier to prove to God that I don't have the necessary gifting for it. Then I'll be off the hook," I reasoned.

From the information I was sent, I discovered how William Cameron Townsend, the founder of Wycliffe Bible Translators, had sold Spanish Bibles in Mexico as a young door-to-door salesman. He was challenged by the question one of the Indians put to him, "If your God really loves us in the way you claim, why doesn't he speak our language?" That made sense to me. The Great Commission, to go into all the world and preach the gospel to everyone, surely implies that we do so in a way that people can understand.

After reading the book *2000 Tongues to Go* which highlights this issue in various ways, I could not help but get on my knees and tell God I was willing to be involved in this task, if that was his will. "Lord," I prayed, "if you think I have the ability to contribute to this ministry so that people will get to read your living word in their own language, then I am ready to be involved. You created me. You know me better than I know myself. You also know which gifts you have given me and which you haven't. Who am I to tell you, Lord, what to do? If you are choosing the wrong person, then at the end of the day that is your responsibility! I am not sure what this means in practice, or what I should do next, but please guide me step by step. Amen."

Not long after that, as I sat down for my evening meal, I opened the *Herrnhuter Losungsbuch*, a German daily devotional book [with a verse from the Old Testament and a verse from the New Testament for each day]. There I read, "The LORD said to Abram, 'Leave your country, your people and your father's household and go to the land I will show you'" (Gen 12:1). That hit me deep in my heart. But I still had my doubts, "This word was for Abraham. I can't just simply take it for me and for my situation." So I prayed, "Lord, if this word is really for me and you want me to be involved in this work for you, then lead me with this word. Amen."

A couple of months later, when my finals were over and I had even had a couple of job interviews, I realised that whether in a career or in missions I would need a good grasp of English. So I decided I should spend a few weeks brushing up my English. A friend gave me the address of a Christian organisation in England, where students could work in exchange for food and lodgings and at the same time practise the language. That sounded perfect for me and so I went to England for six weeks.

Although I had read the information I had received, I was still very surprised when I arrived at Bulstrode to find myself at the International Headquarters of a mission agency. Somehow I had totally missed that in the information! I had not come across WEC International (Worldwide Evangelization for Christ) before.

At mealtimes, which were taken together in the communal dining room, people often asked me, "You come from near Frankfurt, don't you? Do you know the German WEC base in Eppstein?"

"I have often cycled through Eppstein but I have never heard about WEC," I would admit.

"Can you imagine working in missions one day?"

"Yes, I think so," I would reply, "but if I do go into missions, then it would probably be with Wycliffe." It seemed logical to me that if I was to be involved in Bible translation then it was best to do so with an organisation specialising in it.

Bulstrode is a big, old manor house with many wings and long corridors. It also boasts a large park with exotic plants and a small lake. In June the rhododendrons are covered with the most beautiful and fragrant blossom. I shared a room with up to three other language students which meant I got to know people from other cultures. I felt very much at home in this environment and community.

It was a warm summer. Often, early in the morning when the others in the room were still asleep, I would go out into the park and sit under a tree. There I was able to meditate on God's word and pray out loud without disturbing anyone. One June morning, as I sat praying out loud under a tree by the small lake, I heard myself say, "Lord, if you want me to go out with WEC, then confirm it to me while I am still here through that verse you gave me out of Genesis 12:1." I was stunned because that wasn't actually what I wanted! My brain went into overdrive. As I tried to reassure myself, I thought, "My Bible has more than 1000 pages and there are many verses on each page. The likelihood that this exact word will be read during morning devotions is pretty slim!"

That same morning, as I sat in morning devotions, the speaker read the first three verses of Genesis chapter 12! He then went on to speak about something completely different. I was dumbstruck! "How can this be?" I asked myself. "This is no longer a coincidence. He must have read that just for my benefit." I struggled with this thought because I really didn't want to work with WEC. I felt like packing up my things and going home. What should I do?

Suddenly my faith seemed so empty. We often sang "Jesus is Lord!" Was I really letting him be Lord in my life? If he is Lord, then he is also the Lord over missions and over whether, and with which mission agency, I should go. After two days of inner wrestling, I gave up resisting and following my own ideas and got to the point where I could finally say "Yes" to this new direction in my life. With that my inner joy returned.

Three weeks later, back in Germany, I stood in front of the German WEC Headquarters at Hof Häusel in Eppstein. Actually, I was only there to deliver greetings from people at Bulstrode. The wife of the leader opened the door and invited me in. After I had passed on the greetings, we chatted briefly. Then she asked me if God had called me into missions. I ended up telling her everything that had happened. "If God really has called you," she said, "you should probably start preparing and go to Bible school!"

"That's curious," I thought. "At Bulstrode they advised me to build up experience in my career before following my calling. What does God want? I must ask him directly."

I had already received oral confirmation about a position in the Institute for Mathematics and Data Processing at Bad Godesberg and was told the contract would arrive in a few days. I really needed a quick answer from God and decided to fast until I was clear about what I should do. I started that very evening.

The next day I spent time with God in prayer, going through the pros and cons of each possible decision. Whichever way I went, whether job or Bible school, there would be challenges. I needed a clear conviction of the way I should go, guided and affirmed by God. Soon I had the impression that God was showing me that I should be going to Bible school.

The following day I drove to Karlsruhe, the city where I had studied, to collect my graduation certificate, de-register and give up my room keys. At lunchtime I went to the SMD prayer meeting. It was the semester break, but some of the students who had stayed behind to study for their exams were meeting to pray. I spoke with the leaders and asked them to pray with me about this whole thing. We agreed to meet the following evening.

When I met with some of the older SMD students to pray and to ask God for clarity, I told them what had happened in England and said, "Actually, I already feel I have clarity, but I am not going to tell you what it is. I want to be really sure that I have not misheard and I pray that God will tell you the same thing as he has told me!"

With that we began a time of silent and listening prayer. After a while the leader broke the silence, "Let's now share what impressions we have had." One after another they confirmed my own impression. I could hardly believe it and was overjoyed. That was one of the best moments of my life!

Two days later, as I prepared to travel to the Black Forest to meet my parents who were on holiday there to tell them about the new direction in my life, a letter arrived with the contract from the Institute for Mathematics and Data Processing. I was so thankful that it had arrived after I had made my decision! I was putting the last of my things in my travel bag when a gust of wind whooshed through the room. The window banged shut, shattering glass all over the floor. It was as though the enemy was shaking his fist at me, but I wasn't going to let him deter me.

As I hadn't told them I was coming, my parents were most surprised to see me. During the evening meal I explained to them that I had received a definite call into missions. My father immediately told me it was important for me to get experience in a job first. I told him how it all came about and that I was determined to prepare by going to a Bible school in England.

"I wondered whether something like this was going to happen when you went to England," he said, and wanted to know how I expected to finance it.

"My employer will finance it," I assured him. My parents looked at me blankly. "The whole world belongs to God!"

We had many more conversations over the next couple of days. Again and again the question of security and provision came up. I could understand my parents' arguments and their thinking because, from a human point of view, they were right. Of course I could work for a few years and save sufficient to pay for Bible school, but at some point the savings would come to an end, and then I would still have to begin to trust God to look after me. Why not do so straight away?

At night, in my room, I talked to God about it. I questioned my decision but received the same answer again and again that now was the time to decide to be wholehearted in my devotion to him. I realised that "leave your father's household" meant I could not look on my parental home as my ultimate security, a place I could flee to if I no longer knew what to do. It felt so radical. I did not want to cause a rift with my parents. I felt particularly sorry for my mother. I could tell by the pain in her face that she seemed quite upset by it all. I placed even that into God's hands.

Each day we went on long walks together. On the last evening my father said, "We have given you a good education and you have a good job offer. What you do with that is your choice. We respect that. But don't expect that you can just come home and expect us to pick up the pieces when you are stuck and no longer know what to do." I was not surprised to hear this, having been prepared for it in my own thinking. I had that deep assurance that God keeps his promises and would look after me. His word says, "Seek first his kingdom and his righteousness and all these things will be added to you as well" (Matthew 6:33).

# Chapter 2

# God Provides

"Look, there's the New Testament in eight different translations." Toni, a fellow student, pointed to a book. After completing Bible school and spending time as a WEC candidate, I was continuing my preparation for Bible translation work in South Sumatra by doing a course on language learning at the Summer Institute of Linguistics (SIL) in High Wycombe, England. We were on a day trip to Oxford and had gone into a Christian bookshop.

I reached for the thick volume and opened it up. On each side of every double-page spread were four different translations of the same passage. I was excited – this meant you could easily compare eight different translations at once, without having to spend ages going through different books! One of our lecturers had told us about this book and had thoroughly recommended it. It was expensive but, without thinking about it for too long, I made up my mind and bought the book. I had just enough money with me to pay for it, and was delighted with my purchase.

That evening I took stock of my finances and discovered that I didn't have enough money left to pay for my ticket back to Germany. Toni had already booked the tickets, but as I was now a WEC associate, I wanted to keep to their principles and not get into debt. I felt trapped. Had I acted too rashly when I bought the book? Then I remembered how God had looked after me in the past. During my Bible school studies I had always had sufficient, and God had even provided me with enough to pay back my university study grant.

I recalled going to hear a mission presentation by a new missionary from Finland who did not have a supporting sending church. I had felt the urge to put the two notes that were in my purse into the collection plate. When I got back to my room at the Bible school, there was a letter for me containing the exact same sum!

On another occasion, I had been spending my holiday time from Bible school working at Bulstrode. A man from Africa, who was studying in one of the countries behind the Iron Curtain, was working there, too. His financial support was minimal. The rest of the summer workers wanted to encourage him and organised a collection for him. It was only two days before

I was returning to Bible school, so I gladly gave him the rest of my notes. After all, I would only need a bit of change as I had already paid for the coach ticket from London to Liverpool. However, when I had paid for the tube ticket across London, I realised that I had only just enough money left for the bus from the Liverpool bus station back to the Bible school. I felt disappointed that I would have to do without coffee at the service station on the journey. Then, as I sat in the Liverpool coach, I looked in my handbag and found an envelope with a greeting from a German lady with whom I had had a long chat a few days before. It contained £10. I could have a coffee after all! That is what God is like!

This time, though, it was different. I had only myself to blame for finding myself in this mess. I had bought something for myself without thinking about it, even if it was for the Lord's service. The following Sunday the sermon was about God the shepherd who looks after us when we trust his leading. This led me to think of God as a father whose child comes to him with a broken toy and trustingly expects him to fix it. Where else should I turn for help? So I trusted myself and my financial situation into God's hands with the expectation that he would know the way out.

A week later I received a letter from the German mission headquarters. It contained a banker's draft for over DM 100.00 – everything that had come in for my support in the previous month. It was more than I needed for my ticket home and I could even buy a Christmas present for my mother. That is how faithful God is!

# Chapter 3

# Anyone Need a Car?

After completing the language learning course in England, I returned to my parents' home. As I planned my itinerary for the coming months, visiting different churches and people, I realised it would be helpful to have a car. A married man had offered me a car but, needless to say, when he mentioned that his wife was not to find out about it, I declined the offer.

I looked at the adverts for second hand cars in the morning paper and circled various options that were within my price range. But I really didn't know what to look for when buying a car and felt quite helpless. When I asked my father's advice, he looked at me helplessly. "To be honest with you," he said, "I don't know much about it either. I am used to driving new company cars. I am afraid I won't be of much help to you."

"But," I said, "You know more about cars than I do. I've already picked out a few in the paper. Could you just have a look and see if they seem okay?"

I showed him what I had highlighted and we talked about the pros and cons of the cars on offer. I found it exhausting, but helpful. After trying to work out what to do next, I said, "I think I will pop out to see my friend Elisabeth." She was a teacher and her summer holidays were nearly over. Amazingly, she was at home.

"It's so good to see you," she greeted me as she opened the door. As we chatted, she told me she had just ordered a new car. "My old Beetle broke down on the motorway," she said. "I've had the engine replaced, but I want something more reliable for travelling to school. My new car is coming next week, and I want to sell my Beetle. Do you know anyone who needs a car?"

"Yes, actually, I do."

"Who is it?" she asked.

"I myself."

"You?" She looked at me questioningly.

"Yes, for travelling to my meetings. My dad and I have been looking through the newspapers to see what's around but we haven't decided on anything yet."

"Well, if that is the case," she said slowly, and laughed, "I actually wanted to sell the car for DM 1000, but I will give it to you for free. I am supporting you anyway. So you can have the car as soon as the new one arrives. I won't have to worry about selling it, and with the new engine it is actually quite okay." Then she added, more to herself than to me, "Curious how God sorts these things out sometimes."

When I got back home, I greeted my dad with the happy news. He was amazed, and I was glad that I had included him in my deliberations.

# Chapter 4

# Just a Greeting?

When I first arrived in Batu, East Java, I stayed with a German family who lived in a big house in this small town. Nearby was the campus of the Indonesian Missionary Fellowship (IMF) housing the Bible school, a conference hall, music studio and the offices of the various departments of the mission as well as the homes of some of the staff members. The leader's wife introduced me to many of the expatriate and Indonesian workers on campus and explained the roles of the various departments.

One day, as I went to the campus by myself to check the mail, I met an Indonesian lady who seemed familiar to me. Then I remembered I had met her a few days earlier in the office of the missions department, but I couldn't remember her name. I greeted her, saying, "Selamat siang! Good day."

She said, "Where are you going?"

I faltered and stopped. In the few weeks I had been in Batu, I hadn't learnt enough Indonesian to be able to hold a spontaneous conversation, but somehow I managed to explain to her that I was going to the mission campus to check the mail. Then we went on our separate ways.

To be honest I was a bit put out by her question. Was it any of her business where I was going and what I was doing?

A few days later I met the same person on my way to the campus. Remembering the awkward situation of a few days earlier, I decided that this time I was not going to be the one who was questioned.

"Where are you going?" I asked quickly.

"There!" came the prompt reply, and she pointed with her chin in the direction from which I had just come. And with that the brief encounter was over.

"It's as easy as that," I thought as I walked on.

Years later, in the village in southern Sumatra, I came across this greeting again and again. People were always asking each other where they had come from and where they were going. Then I remembered that in my home area in Germany there was a similar greeting with an equally meaningless answer. It was, after all, just that – a greeting.

# Chapter 5

# Javanese Politeness

"It is better if you say it this way."

I was having an Indonesian lesson with my Javanese language teacher who was looking at my homework. He was a lecturer at the teacher training college in Malang, East Java, about half an hour's drive from Batu.

"Is it wrong?" I asked him.

"It is better if you say it this way," he repeated.

"So it is wrong?" I asked again.

His answer was the same, "It is better to say it the other way."

I knew that in each language there are various ways of expressing the same thing, some more polite than others. I had also heard that in Javanese the ways of expressing something is dependent on whether you are speaking to people below your rank, of equal rank, of higher rank or even of titled rank. But I was learning Indonesian not Javanese, and as far as I was aware, it wasn't like that in Indonesian. I wanted to know for sure so asked, "Is it wrong or is the other simply a better way of putting it?"

My teacher stuck to his answer, "The other is better."

I was still not fully convinced that we had got to the bottom of it so I said, "I know that there are polite and less polite ways of expressing something. Is what I have written wrong or is the other simply better?"

"It is better if you say it differently," he responded with a polite smile.

I was close to despair. Somehow we seemed to be talking at cross purposes. After discussing the matter some more, I said, "Do you mean that I can say it this way, but that the other is just a better way?"

He replied, "You can't really say it that way."

In other words, it really was wrong. But, as a polite Javanese teacher, he hadn't wanted to discourage me, his student, by saying that what I had written was wrong.

To be honest, I knew I wouldn't easily get used to this way of correcting!

If my teacher was so reluctant to correct my grammar, I wondered what he would be like correcting my pronunciation! I had heard some of the other expatriates speak with a strong foreign accent and I really didn't want to get used to wrong pronunciation. But what do you do if the language teacher is not brave enough to correct you properly?

A few days later I asked my teacher what my pronunciation was like. He praised it, saying I was easily understood and much better than one of his Japanese students. I knew who he meant because that man's pronunciation was particularly poor. I soon realized we had the same problem that my teacher was reluctant to point out my mistakes. I had to learn to ask about them in a different way. So I worked out what I thought were my weak areas and which sounds are different in German from Indonesian. The obvious ones were the plosives. "What about my pronunciation of P, T and K?" I asked. "Could they be better?"

Much to my surprise he responded readily. "Yes," he said. "They are still quite hard and should really be softer."

In Indonesian, unlike in German, plosives are unaspirated, so without a strong push of air following them, they sound softer. I was a bit disappointed that my pronunciation wasn't as good as I had thought, but at the same time I was encouraged that I was managing to express myself better and get a clear answer to my questions.

Then I asked him, "Are there other areas we should work on?"

"Yes, the 'ng' sounds as in 'dengan' (with)."

"What about it?"

"It doesn't really belong to the first syllable, but with the second; so it's not 'deng-an' but 'de-ngan'."

"This is getting better and better," I thought to myself. "He really is correcting me! I must make the most of this opportunity!"

"What about my vowels?" I wanted to know.

"They are quite good," he said encouragingly, "unlike those of your American and Japanese colleagues." His mischievous grin seemed entirely genuine.

# Chapter 6

# Hospital Visiting

"Kjersti would like you to visit her," the mission leader told me. "Would you be able to go on Saturday?"

Kjersti was a Norwegian colleague, about my age, who had been in Batu about a year longer than I had. She was with the Norwegian Lutheran Mission and her role was to teach the Norwegian children and to work with a project for local children. Each Monday evening she had invited me, together with a lady from Switzerland and another from Finland who were both also in their first term, to dinner. Over delicious homemade bread, we would share our experiences and adventures in this foreign culture and pray for one another. Those had been very precious hours as we encouraged and built one another up.

A week earlier, Kjersti had been admitted to the Baptist hospital in Kediri with a high temperature. Kediri is about three hours' drive from Batu but significantly longer by public transport. I caught the early bus from Malang to Kediri which passed through Batu just after 6 am. It was already light, and a number of pickup trucks were coming down from the mountains, laden with vegetables for the market. When the bus appeared from the opposite direction, I held out my hand and it stopped for me to get on. It was already quite full so I was glad to get a seat.

As the bus travelled up the winding road to Pujon through constantly changing scenery, there were wonderful views over Batu and the surrounding mountains. Below us we could see Songgokerto, a leisure complex with hotels and swimming pools. It was the first time I had travelled this route and really enjoyed the constantly changing scenery. When we reached the top we stopped briefly and a few more passengers boarded the bus. From there we travelled downhill along the gently winding road, past small streams and over rickety bridges. It was not long before I started to chat with the lady sitting next to me.

"Where are you going?" she asked me.

"To Kediri, to the hospital, to visit a friend," I explained.

"Why don't you go in your own car and get your chauffeur to drive you?" she wanted to know.

"I don't have one," I replied.

"Masak! Really?"

It seemed strange to her to meet a white lady who did not live in a big bungalow with many servants and had neither car nor chauffeur. Like many Indonesians she was under the impression that all white people were rich and could afford anything they wanted. The fact that we had been able to afford to travel to their country was evidence enough of our wealth.

When she got off the bus a man sat down beside me. I was reading a booklet and he asked what I was reading.

"The Gospel of John" I told him. "Would you like it?"

"No thanks. I've already read it."

"Are you a Christian too?"

"No, I am a Muslim." he replied. "Mohammed is the fulfilment of Jesus' teachings."

I looked at him, puzzled. "What do you mean?"

"That's what we believe," he said. "Jesus pointed clearly to Mohammed. He talked about someone who would come after him who would lead men into all truth. He meant Mohammed by that."

We had a long conversation about religion but the man remained convinced that he was right about Jesus and his teachings. I was glad when he got off the bus! I had been in Indonesia for little more than a year and was finding it still difficult to have conversations like that.

Soon we left the mountains behind and large rice fields stretched out for miles on either side of the road. It was also getting markedly warmer. It was almost midday when we arrived at the bus station in Kediri. From there it was just a few minutes' walk to the hospital.

Kjersti had a private room with an en-suite bathroom. This meant I could be with her in her room without disturbing other patients. She was so happy to have someone with her from her own cultural circle and with whom she could speak English. She told me about her experiences in the hospital and especially how the Indonesian nurses all wanted to touch her white skin. "They say it is so soft," she said, "and then they pinch it!" She felt so defenceless and was so weak she couldn't make the few steps to the bathroom by herself. She couldn't even hold her Bible to read it. I helped her as much as I could.

"Please come back next week," she begged me as I left just before 4 pm to get the last bus back to Batu. I promised I would. I sat in the bus and dozed. Suddenly, in the middle of nowhere, the bus ground to a halt. Smoke was pouring out from under the bonnet. We all got off the bus immediately. The driver had a look at the engine and decided there was nothing he could do. We stood or sat at the side of the road, the rice fields stretching out for miles on either side, and waited patiently. Thankfully it was not raining. There was still a good three hours' drive to Batu and some passengers chose to continue their journey in smaller vehicles. Most people around me were chatting in Javanese, which I didn't understand.

"How will we get from here to Batu?" I asked a passenger in Indonesian.

"Another bus is coming," he told me.

Well, if they had called for another one, then it was best to wait. Meanwhile it was getting dark and the mosquitoes were starting to bite. At last a bus arrived. It was already full, but everyone tried to squeeze inside. I was a bit hesitant, but didn't want to be left behind standing alone in the dark, so I squeezed myself in along with everybody else. We had to pull in our stomachs to be able to close the door. When we reached the mountains it started to rain. At each bend in the road the bus swayed dangerously from one side to the other. The passengers fell on each another but we were standing too close together to fall right over. Standing in this hopelessly overcrowded bus, holding on tightly to a bar and desperately trying to keep upright as the bus took the bends in the road, I let the events of the day run through my mind. Instead of allowing this dreadful journey home to upset me, I was filled with overwhelming thankfulness that I was able to stand in this bus on my own two feet and that I was not lying in a hospital bed, helpless and weak, like my colleague.

"Thank you, Lord, for this experience."

# Chapter 7

# Paper Wars

The Indonesian leader of the IMF called me into her office. "I think you should go to Sumatra as soon as possible," she told me. I had to contain my delight so it would not to be too obvious.

I'd been in Indonesia about 18 months and was still in Batu, East Java. As well as doing my orientation and language learning, I had been teaching German missionary children and giving English lessons to Indonesian colleagues. When I had first arrived in Indonesia, I was told that I had to count on being at the base of the Indonesian Missionary Fellowship (IMF), my indigenous sponsoring organisation, for about two years before I could move to southern Sumatra, where I wanted to translate the New Testament into the Serawai language. Now I had the green light to prepare for the move there. What a surprise and what a delight!

I soon discovered it was not that straightforward. First of all I had to extend my visa which was due to run out in about five months. Thankfully, the Indonesian office of the IMF was able to sort all that out.

After my visa extension was granted, the papers I needed to permit me to move to Sumatra went from one office to the next, first in the Province of East Java and later in the capital, Jakarta. I had to practise a lot of patience and bided my time by helping out in various offices. It took a whole year before I finally held the confirmation documents from Jakarta in my hands. I was overjoyed. The rest of the formalities that need to be sorted out on a local level shouldn't be that difficult – or so I thought. Then I realised that my passport needed to be renewed so that I would be able to apply for the next visa extension.

"Send it to the Embassy by registered post," the German mission leader advised. "That's what we all do. You will have it back in two weeks."

I was not unduly worried when my passport was not back after two weeks. However, when I checked it out, I discovered it had never arrived at the Embassy. Since the move from one island to another had to be entered in my passport by the immigration office, there was no way I could be without it.

I couldn't find my copy of the proof of posting anywhere, but the post office clerk was very helpful and finally managed to unearth a copy of the proof of posting form. She sent an enquiry to Jakarta immediately, but could do no more to help me.

I didn't hold out much hope and applied for a new passport straight away. When, three weeks later, I found a thick envelope from the German Embassy in my mail box, I was very surprised because it contained my old passport! Oh well, rather the old one than none at all!

In the meantime the month of Ramadan, the month of fasting, had begun. As many of the office employees were either absent or too tired to work, this affected the speed in which any formalities were processed. But at least I could now see the end of the tunnel – I would soon be able to move to Bengkulu. I didn't have much to pack, really only my personal things. However, realising that I needed to start the process of extending my visa again, and that once I was in Bengkulu there would be no one on hand to help me, I asked the IMF missions office to explain clearly to me all of the registration formalities. Then, all of a sudden, things happened very quickly.

Because the month of fasting was ending, all regular flights were fully booked. There were, however, some special flights with available seats, and I was able to book a ticket from Malang to Jakarta where I hoped to meet up with my colleague Renate, who was on her way from Sumatra to Germany for a home visit. I needed just one last letter from the police. Amazingly, it was ready and waiting when we called for it on our way to the airport! What a miracle!

# Chapter 8

# Finally in Sumatra!

At last I was sitting in the plane to Jakarta. I closed my eyes and breathed deeply. Now I could begin to relax. Transferring my documents to Sumatra had been hindered by so much red tape – all in all it had taken a whole year! Then everything seemed to happen very quickly.

That morning I had said goodbye to various Indonesian friends on the IMF campus and at lunchtime some friends took me to the airport. It was all rather chaotic – first of all we had to go to the police station to collect one last letter and then to the travel agency to collect the ticket I had booked by phone. It hadn't been printed out and the agency was still waiting for the form from the flight company! So I waited. A quick look at the clock as I left the travel agency made me realise I should already be checking in as the flight was due to leave in an hour!

However, when we arrived at the airport in Malang half an hour later, the plane had not yet arrived. What a relief! A good hour later the announcement came through that the flight was cancelled. Thankfully I was not alone as I had to return to the travel agency with my ticket. The travel agent was able to reserve a place for me on the last flight from Surabaya to Jakarta, due to leave in about three hours. I got a place in a shared taxi which spent the first hour of the journey driving through the town collecting passengers. It was afternoon and there was a lot of traffic on the roads. Half an hour before the flight departure we finally arrived at the airport in Surabaya. I paid for my ticket, checked in and boarded straight away.

The first leg of the journey was behind me, even though it had been full of obstacles. As we took off into the evening sky my heart said, "Thank you Lord." Then, as it was the time to break the fast, I even got a snack on that flight.

Renate was waiting for me when I arrived at my accommodation in Jakarta later that evening. How good that we were able to have a day together to talk about aspects of the work I was about to embark on.

My plane to Bengkulu was due to leave at 7 am the next morning. I arrived at the airport on time, checked in and sat down in the waiting room. It was all starting to feel very real. I was now really on the way to the village of Napal Melintang to begin the task I had come to do – to translate the New

Testament into the language of the Serawai people. Suddenly I felt very small and insignificant. "What on earth have I let myself in for?" I wondered. "What will happen to me? Will I cope?"

There was still about an hour before the flight, time enough to read the Bible and to pray. Ignoring the people and music around me, I opened my German devotional guide. The verse for the day was 2 Corinthians 3:5b+6a "our competence is from God. He has made us competent as ministers of a new covenant."

It was as though God was speaking directly into my situation. I realised that it was not about what I was capable of doing but that it was God who would enable me. He had promised to do so because He had assigned me my task, to serve Him and to take the good news of a relationship with God to the people in Bengkulu. I would do my bit, and he would make it grow. I was both encouraged and in awe. Even at 6 am in the airport in Jakarta I was able to experience God's presence.

"Thank you, Lord, for your word. Yes, I know that I am not able to do it on my own, nor do I have to. Thank you that you can and will enable and empower me. Amen."

It was a good flight. The morning was bright and the forest and mountains of southern Sumatra were clearly visible. Below me, as the plane turned above the city of Bengkulu, I could see the old English fortress and the waves along the long sandy beach.

Edna, my American colleague, who had only recently moved to Bengkulu with her family, picked me up at the airport. The roads were almost deserted as it was the first day of Eid, Idul Fitri, the big feast following the month of fasting.

I spent a couple of days with the American family and together we visited neighbours and wished them a blessed feast. Everyone seemed happy to see us and honoured that we had visited them on their day of celebration. Late in the afternoon we went to Bengkulu's beach of fine, white sand and went for a swim in the strong waves of the Indian Ocean. It was great fun!

The time finally came for me to travel on to the village of Napal Melintang, south of Bengkulu, my place of work for the next few years. I drove Renate's car and, although only 145 kilometres, the journey took me about three and a half hours because of the many potholes and bends in the road. Despite being the first time I had driven on the left-hand side of the road, everything went smoothly.

I turned off the tarmac coastal road and drove the last 7 km on the red mud track to the village. The people recognised Renate's car and shouted greetings to me as I drove past. As the road dipped downhill, the Pino valley opened up in front of me. In the distance the wide river with its big mean-ders glinted in the afternoon sun. The valley was covered in rice fields and I could see the hills on the other side of the river. I spotted a grove of palm trees under which some of the forty or so village houses were built. I had finally arrived at my destination! Joy flooded through me and a thought ran through my mind, "This is now home!"

As I stopped in front of the garage a crowd of children came running up. Eagerly they helped me carry my bags up the slope to my house, where I was greeted by Immanuel, a trainee Bible school student on his practical placement, and his wife.

Yes, finally, I had arrived at my destination. But it was really only the beginning!

Part 2

# First Impressions of Village Life

# Chapter 9

# The Village

A year earlier, Renate, my co-worker, had invited me to visit her in the village in order to familiarise myself with the situation and I was able to spend several weeks there.

Napal Melintang is seven kilometres from the main coastal road along a wide, red mud track. Its 65 houses line the road and village square. About a kilometre away across the rice fields are the 15 houses of the hamlet of Suka Merindu where the Christian primary school is located. Napal Melintang itself has a state primary school, a prayer house for Muslims and a small church. Although 99.9% of the surrounding population is Muslim, there is a small Christian congregation of about 40 families in the village.

The traditional houses are made of wood and are built on stilts. At the front of each house is a big veranda where guests are readily entertained. The kitchen, where meals are cooked on an open fire, is usually an extension at the back of the house and is built of bamboo, which is less combustible than wood. Firewood is stored under the house, and animals, such as chickens, ducks and goats, are kept there as well. The roofs are predominantly made from corrugated iron, but the kitchen roofs tend to be thatched with leaves, making it easier for the smoke to draw away. Some houses have a well at the back, but many village people go to the public spring for water. Coconut palms, banana plants and a variety of fruit trees grow in among the houses.

The villagers are all farmers and even the teacher works on his field in the afternoons. The village is about a kilometre from the Pino River. The people grow rice in the river valley during the rainy season, and peanuts, corn and vegetables in the dry season. Once in a while the river bursts its banks and floods the fields. In the hills behind the village there are several coffee groves, many fruit trees and a lot of forest – home to many monkeys.

Renate also worked with WEC International. She was a nurse and midwife, and for over ten years had been providing the people of Napal Melintang with medical assistance. In the mornings she ran a clinic, which basically consisted of a consultation room equipped with a medicine cupboard and camp bed. Between the coastal road and the village there was a state-run health clinic, where a doctor was available, but Renate often saw between 80 and 120 patients in a day. Many of her patients travelled up to 50 kilometres to be treated by her.

When I arrived in the village in the summer of 1984, the clinic was closed as Renate was away for six months on home leave in Germany. I stayed in her house, together with an Indonesian trainee Bible school student and his wife.

Renate's big house had been built by the villagers. Unlike their houses it was not built on stilts but flat on the ground with a cement floor. The walls of the house were plastered with cement to the height of a metre and above that the walls, as well as the ceiling, were made of wooden planks. There was no glass in the windows but only wire mesh to keep out the flies, and shutters that were closed when it got dark. The three bedrooms, guest room, the spacious living room and the consultation room for the clinic were set out in the shape of an L. In front of the consultation room was a covered veranda which served as a waiting area for patients. The kitchen and dining room were in a separate building at the back of the main house. The roof of the house was made from corrugated iron. This meant that whenever there was a tropical rainstorm, the water running off the roof into the gutters was channelled into the large, cemented water basin in the bathroom, or into drums set up all around the house. In that way we usually had enough water. Behind the house there was a diesel-run generator which was started up every evening. As it did not only supply electricity to our house, but to 10 other houses as well, the men of the village took care of the generator. I was thankful for the electric light as I found it difficult to read by the weak light of candles and oil lamps, and the gas lamps provided unwelcome additional heat in the tropical climate.

Each morning and evening the villagers went by our house on the main path leading to their fields. We often asked them what they were carrying in their baskets and sometimes they would offer us some of their vegetables.

Some of the village grandmothers would visit us in the evenings and stay overnight. In this culture, no women, especially unmarried ones, are left alone in a house at night. Usually, it was the same ladies who came, and as they brought with them the latest village news, we were kept informed of what was happening in the community.

The first thing they did when they arrived was to spread out their grass mats on the living room floor and make themselves comfortable. Much to their delight, we sat with them and played Ludo, which Renate had taught them. Later on, as we chatted, I would take out my notebook and a pencil and note down the new words and expressions I heard. Sometimes I thought up word games, for example finding opposites such as hot and cold, long and short, fat and thin, or pairs that belong together such as day and night or man and woman. They always enjoyed teaching me in this way. They also taught me how to weave baskets. They explained to me, too, how to make good coffee. This included harvesting it, the production of the coffee powder and the correct way to serve it. All this was precious information for the impending translation work.

# Chapter 10

# Heart Language

"Are you coming? The ceremony has already started."

It was still early in the morning and I'd only been in the village a few days.

Many traditional weddings take place in the months following the May rice harvest. Everyone has time to celebrate, and as the rice stores are full, celebrations can take place out of the abundance of the harvest.

That day the daughter of the village elder, Pak Anil, was getting married. The village celebrated it with a traditional wedding *bimbang*[4] . Pak Anil was one of the first Christians in the village and, even though the groom came from a Muslim family, he had planned a Christian marriage ceremony in the late morning. Pastor Rusdi, who was also a Serawai man and came originally from Siginim, had been invited to conduct the service.

The wedding ceremony started at 7 o'clock in the morning with the bride dancing around the water buffalo which was to be slaughtered for the feast. As I got closer, I could hear the sound of the *lintang*[5] . When I reached the village square, I saw lots of people standing in a circle. In the middle of the circle, tied to a pole, was the water buffalo with its eyes and ears covered with mud so that it could not take in its surroundings. The bride was wearing a *sarong*[6] and a deep red velvet jacket, the edges of which were embroidered with gold. She had a tall crown on her head and her face was covered with a deep red veil, held in place by the crown. She spread out her arms and danced with small, rhythmic steps around the water buffalo. Some women, dressed for the feast, joined her.

I had heard that the point of this ceremony was to put the ancestors into a good mood so that they would bless the wedding and the young couple. However, as the family members were Christians, they wanted to leave out those elements, but had not wanted to cut out the dance around the water buffalo

---

[4]   A *bimbang* is the big, traditional wedding - a water buffalo is slaughtered and in the evening there is dancing for the youth as well as the men.

[5]   The *lintang* is a musical instrument made up of four or five tin bells, which are hit rhythmically with a bamboo stick to make a sound.

[6]   A *sarong* is the traditional round cloth people wear. It is made of a colourful batik cloth for ladies and of a checked cloth for men.

totally because it was considered an important part of the wedding day. The dance was not drawn out – the men were standing by, ready with their sharpened machetes to slaughter and cut up the animal. In the days running up to the wedding, the women had collected and prepared the different ingredients, spices and seasoning needed for the various dishes. As soon as the first cuts of meat were delivered, the women, who were sitting at a log which served as a gigantic cutting board, cut them up into small pieces. The fires were lit and everyone seemed to know what they could do to help.

For the Christian wedding ceremony, which was held two hours later, the bride was dressed in white. My colleague Renate had once brought a wedding dress with a veil from Germany and now every bride could borrow it for the church ceremony. If the dress was too big or too long, it was taken in and adjusted accordingly, or held in place with safety pins.

The church was well attended. The members of the congregation who were not involved in cooking were there as well as many of the invited guests, including the relatives of the groom. It soon became clear that most of the congregation had never been to a church service before. The service was held in the national language – Indonesian. The readings were taken from the Indonesian Bible. Pastor Rusdi preached in Indonesian as he had been taught at Bible school, but most people didn't even try to understand what he was saying. They chatted to one another, and the noise level got louder and louder. Pastor Rusdi certainly had his work cut out! But then he told a story to illustrate a point and changed from Indonesian to his mother tongue, Serawai. The atmosphere changed dramatically. The guests become as quiet as mice. No-one wanted to miss a word.

After the service it was time for the feast. To eat, the guests sat on mats that had been spread out on the wooden floor at the front of the house. In the back of the house the women sat in front of big baskets of rice and bowls of vegetables and meat, and served the food onto plates. Each guest received three plates – one with rice, one with a few bits of meat and a lot of sauce and one with vegetables. Many additional plates were brought in, laden with various meat dishes, vegetables and rice, for people to have seconds.

The men ate first, the young, single men were serving the food. When a group of men had finished eating, the boys took the plates away and the next group of men had their turn. Last of all, it was the turn of the women and children to eat.

As a guest of honour I was invited to eat with the bride and groom in the wedding room which was decorated with colourful batik cloths. The couple sat on a mattress in front of a four-poster double bed which filled most of the room. Some of the bride's girl friends kept her company. Together with the other guests of honour I sat on the floor, pressed against the wall, my legs curled tightly under me. Then the food was served. The wedding couple and the guests of honour received a bit of every dish. Although the space in the middle of the room was very small, a veritable mountain of plates full of various delicacies appeared as plates were placed on the edges of other plates. Very little air came in through the small window so it got hotter and hotter in the room.

The feast was a long drawn out affair. Those of us who were guests of honour were able to take our time and did not have to hurry to get up and leave in order to make space for other guests. There was plenty of time for conversation. Finally, coffee was served along with homemade pastries and sweets.

The celebrations continued in the evening. The young people had their own dance event on the village square and others came from neighbouring villages to meet up with friends or to make new ones. The *lintang* determined the beat and the young people danced a little like the bride had in the morning, but in pairs, and with only one couple dancing at a time. To the uninitiated observer this may appear boring, but for the young people it is often at such occasions that new couples get together.

I found the men's dance event much more interesting. The men sat on their mats in a big circle around the dance floor where solo as well as paired dancers would perform. Someone played the violin; several men had tambourines and gave the beat. With traditional cloths in his hands the dancer moved in time to the music, often stamping loudly on the wooden floor with his feet. My favourite dance was the plate dance. During that dance the dancer held a plate flat on each hand and made dramatic moves with his arms or with his whole body, without dropping the plates. At the same time, using a thimble on his middle finger, he tapped out the beat on the plate.

The women sat slightly apart, making coffee for the guests and chatting. And so the celebrations continued until the early hours of the morning. I sat with them and enjoyed what was for me a new experience in a strange environment.

That night, as I let the day run through my mind again, I realised the experience during the sermon had left a deep impression on me. Somehow it confirmed what I wanted to do here. I had sometimes asked myself if it was actually necessary to translate the Bible into the Serawai language as it already existed in Indonesian. Most of the men and women aged 35 and under had gone to school and could read and write Indonesian. Yet this event had shown me again that the national tongue does not touch a person's heart as deeply as their own mother tongue.

Chapter 11

# Where Do I Fit in?

About three weeks later, there was yet another Christian wedding in the village. This time it was not a traditional wedding. Instead, the family had arranged something special and had organised a real band for the evening. The men had even put up a temporary wooden bandstand for the occasion.

Two students from the Bible school in Batu, East Java, who were doing their year's practical placement here in the Province of Bengkulu, were among the guests. I knew them from my time in Batu and had met up with them in Bengkulu on my way to the village a few weeks earlier. One of them, Agus, came from Java, and the other one, Frederik, was from the Province of Manado, in northern Sulawesi, at the other end of the country. While we waited for the other guests to arrive, we chatted animatedly about our first impressions and experiences with the culture of southern Sumatra. Agus, the Javanese, was finding the people of Sumatra often rather rough and far too direct. I had to admit that I felt I got on better with the Sumatran culture than with Javanese ways.

After a while I realised that it was probably not acceptable for me to be seen spending the evening in the company of those two young men. I had begun to notice that the villagers got together in groups, depending on age or status, so I took my leave of the two students and looked for the group of unmarried ladies. These were mainly young girls, mostly still teenagers, who really didn't know what to do with me and giggled about everything I said. I soon realised I was not wanted among them.

I tried joining my peer group. Most of them had a baby in a sling over their shoulder, and a toddler hanging on to their skirts. The conversation revolved around family issues: bringing up children, cooking, pregnancy, children's illnesses and so on. I found it difficult to join in. We didn't have much in common and we really didn't warm to one another. So I went along to the grandmothers. They knew me and gladly took me into their circle. I felt most comfortable in their midst. This was obviously the place for me to be, even though I was only in my early thirties.

# Chapter 12

# Compliments in Serawai

There was a call at the front of the house, so I went to open the door. It was an older man.

"*Selamat siang, Pak*[7]," I greeted him and asked him where he was from and what he wanted.

"I am from the other side of the river and need some fever medicine."

By this the local people usually meant malaria tablets.

"Unfortunately the nurse is not here," I replied. Renate was still on home leave in Germany. The man was visibly disappointed.

"Can't you give me the medicine?" he pleaded.

It was unusual for a patient to ask for tablets. Most of the time, they wanted an injection and were even disappointed when they only received tablets. I could give him his tablets and then get on with my work. But then I felt this was a good opportunity for me to practice my newly-learned Serawai.

"Are you ill?" I asked in Serawai.

"It is my wife."

"And where is she?"

"At home, across the river."

I suspected that the malaria tablets were not really what the woman needed and so I continued with my questions.

"Does she have any shivers?" As I only knew the Indonesian word for that and was not sure if he understood me, I used the relevant actions to describe what I meant.

"No," he replied. Just as I thought – it was probably not malaria after all.

"Does she have a cold?"

"No."

"A cough?"

"No."

"Does she have diarrhoea?"

---

[7]  *Selamat siang* is an Indonesian greeting reflecting the time of day, and means 'Good day'. *Pak* is the formal way of addressing a man, meaning something like 'Mister' or 'Sir'.

"No."

I was stumped. There had to be a reason for the fever and, as far as I was aware, I had gone through most of the symptoms associated with temperatures.

"How long has she had the fever?" I asked.

"Nearly three weeks."

"Are there any other symptoms?"

"Yes, she is really yellow."

Then it dawned on me: the woman had hepatitis.

I recalled that when I was a child my father had had hepatitis. I seemed to remember there was no medication for it and that he had not been allowed to eat much fat but had eaten a lot of *quark*[8]. When I was still in Java, I had bought the book *Where There is No Doctor* in Indonesian, in order to be able to help local people with their illnesses. I got out the book and read to him what it said about hepatitis. I wasn't sure that I understood everything, and that he, as a simple farmer, had understood any more than I had. So I tried to explain it to him again in simple Indonesian, mixing in any Serawai words I knew. He confirmed that the fever had gone down when his wife turned yellow. I explained to him that she should not eat anything fried, but should eat a lot of fresh fruit.

After I had explained everything to him for the third time, he asked, "Where are you actually from?"

"I am from Germany. I am German."

"No, you are Indonesian."

"No," I replied. "I really am German, just like the nurse."

"That's not possible," he insisted. "You are Indonesian."

"What makes you say that?" I asked.

"It is just that you speak our language."

---

[8] *Quark* is a German low fat dairy product, a kind of curd cheese.

Chapter 13

# An Unsuccessful Hunt?

Christian and his friend, two young theology students from Germany, visited me for a couple of days. They were on a fact-finding tour of Indonesia, visiting different missionaries to find out how they did their work. I was looking forward to the change and to having the opportunity to speak German again. They arrived in the village on a Friday afternoon and a crowd of young people and children accompanied them to my house. After the initial greetings, I explained about their accommodation.

"Unfortunately, I don't have a spare room for you as the trainee students from Batu are staying in my guest room. I have arranged for you to stay with our neighbours who have sons your age. You can sleep there, but will come to my house for meals. Later this afternoon I'll take you to meet the family. We also have to visit the village head to register your arrival." They were happy with the arrangement as it meant they would meet local people.

Before we went to the neighbours' house, I showed them the facilities behind my house so that they could freshen up after their journey. "Just dip the jug into the big basin, take water out and pour it over yourselves. The water will run off through the hole over there."

My neighbours had a lovely wooden house, built on thick pillars and with a large veranda where guests were received and entertained during the day. I introduced my guests to the family who gave them a warm welcome. We continued on through the village to the house of the village head.

"I want to register my two guests," I told him.

"Where are they from?"

"From Germany."

"How long do they want to stay?"

"They want to stay two days here in the village."

They handed over their passports, which the village head studied intently. Then he got up, went into his house and returned with a big book and pen. He was a simple farmer and, as he made opening the book look complicated, I realised that he had not done this often. I helped him find the correct information and he entered the names, ages, nationality and passport numbers into the book. It took quite a long time until both entries were ready to be signed. Dusk had fallen, and it would soon be dark for dusk only

44

lasts a short while in the tropics. We quickly took our leave as we hadn't brought a torch.

The next morning I drove the young men to the police station in Manna, to register them there as well. On the way back, we took a detour to the mouth of the Pino River where the beach is stony. We had taken big buckets with us and filled them with stones to fill in a mud hole on the village road. Everyone helped and the small boot of the car was soon filled. An occasional load of stones helped to keep the track passable.

During lunch I told Christian and his friend that some of the youth in our neighbourhood often went hunting for wild boar on Saturday afternoons.

"Would you like to go with them?" I asked. "Both of my dogs go along, and they even get a cut of the booty – well, I get it of course."

"Why not? That would be something different." They were both very excited at the prospect.

"Make sure nothing happens to them," I told the young people when they came to pick up my guests. "They have never done anything like this before and they don't know the area."

"What kind of weapons do we use to hunt?" one of them asked the village lads.

"Spears."

"And how do you do that? What do you have to aim for?"

"It doesn't matter where you hit the boar, whether on the head or on the tail," one of the young men explained, "as long as you hit it."

"They should enjoy this," I thought, "but I hope they all get home safely."

I was thankful to have the afternoon to myself, as my whole body ached and I had a temperature. I was sure I was coming down with something. I had taken some aspirin which kept me going. Being on my own gave me the opportunity to have a nap. Late that afternoon, when there was still no sign of the hunters' return, I began to worry and wondered whether it had been such a good idea of mine to send my two guests hunting. Dusk was already falling when I saw them on the path to my house. I went outside to greet them.

It was clear they were both exhausted but they did not seem the slightest bit discouraged. "No contact with the enemy," they told me, "but, nevertheless, there are two wounded soldiers."

"What happened?" I asked, worried.

Christian pulled up his trouser leg to reveal blood running down his calf. "That's thanks to the leeches."

The second wounded soldier was one of my dogs. The leeches must have got him as well. Later, when the fellows had washed and the injuries been attended to, we chatted over our meal. I asked them if they really had not seen any wild boar. "It would have been a miracle if we had," Christian exclaimed. "We started off by walking through the village. When they saw that we were going hunting, the entire village youth joined us. They made so much noise that any wild boar would have taken flight long before we had the chance to get anywhere near it!"

The next morning I took my guests to the church service. The previous week it had been announced that one of the two students would preach. Christian had agreed to preach and I translated. When we arrived at the church it was unusually full. Many of the youth, who normally only came to church on special occasions, were already sitting expectantly on the benches. The wild boar hunt was obviously more of a success than we had thought!

# Chapter 14

# Diesel in Plastic Bags

"I wonder how much diesel this car actually needs?"
That question had bothered me ever since my arrival in the village. I was really concerned about how far I could drive before the tank was empty and the car stopped. Throughout the whole of the province the only petrol stations with real petrol pumps were located in the town of Bengkulu, about 145 kilometres from Napal Melintang. Elsewhere you could buy petrol from small street depots which were equipped with several big metal barrels filled with petrol, diesel or oil. Fuel was sold by the litre – or by the canister – and naturally at slightly higher prices than in Bengkulu. We kept four 20-litre canisters, which we filled up at a real petrol station, to keep us going.

I was soon to find the answer to my question!

The following day I had to drive to the airport in Bengkulu to pick up Renate and Ursula, who had had a lot of experience in Bible translation in Indonesia. Since both were from Germany, I was looking forward to seeing them again. On the way to Bengkulu I noticed the petrol indicator going further and further down and pretty much reaching the empty mark. Usually, that means there was another 30 to 40 kilometres' worth of petrol left in the tank – at least that was the case with my Beetle in Germany.

As I drove past a petrol station in Bengkulu, I noticed there was a long line of cars queuing up for petrol. After a 3-hour drive I was feeling tired and couldn't face joining a long queue. I decided I would fill up with diesel the next morning on my way to the airport. The next morning the queue was no shorter. "There's no way I can join the queue now," I told myself, "or I shall be late getting to the airport. I'll get the fuel on the way back. I'm sure we will manage these next 15 kilometres." So I continued on to the airport.

The flight from Jakarta landed on time and we are all so happy to see one other again. We put the luggage in the open cargo area at the back of the car and set off. We had a lot to tell each other and I totally forgot the empty petrol tank. All of a sudden the car jolted to a halt and the engine cut out. I just about managed to manoeuvre the car to the side of the road. We got out and opened the bonnet to work out what was wrong. None of us really understood much about cars but we pretended we did.

Not long afterwards a *microlet*[9] stopped. It was full of passengers, but the driver got out and offered to help these three white ladies. He soon realised that our problem was lack of fuel.

"Didn't you get diesel?" Renate asked me, horrified.

"I'll go to the petrol station and get some," I offered quickly. Then I remembered I had left the empty canisters at the house to leave space for the luggage.

I travelled on the *microlet* to the petrol station where I told the petrol attendant that my car was stuck about seven kilometres away and that I needed some diesel.

"Where is your canister?" he asked.

"I didn't bring one. Couldn't you lend me your bucket?"

"My bucket?" He shook his head vigorously. "No way. I need it here." Maybe he was afraid I wouldn't take it back.

"How am I supposed to transport the fuel?"

"In plastic bags?" he suggested.

"Plastic bags?! Where am I going to get those from?"

"Over there," he said and pointed with his chin to the other side of the road. I couldn't see any plastic bags.

"Where?"

"There, at the kiosk."

I bought four big plastic bags. We put one bag inside another and the petrol attendant carefully filled the two resulting containers with a few litres of diesel. I was just wondering how I was going to get the precious fuel back to our car without spilling any, when a bus drove up to get fuel.

"Where are you going," I asked the driver.

"To Manna."

"Can I get a lift with you for a bit? My car is stuck about seven kilometres from here by the side of the road."

He grinned and nodded his head. "No worries."

I held my bags as though they contained fragile and precious objects. When I arrived back at the car, Renate's first question was, "Where's the fuel?"

"Here!" I said proudly, holding up the bags. "Hold this one for a minute," I said, and handed one of the bags to Ursula. I made a hole in the bottom of the other bag and let the diesel run into the empty tank. I did the same with the second bag. Renate turned a screw to let the air out of the pipes. She started the car, the engine jumped back into life and we continued on our way to the petrol station.

---

[9]  *Microlet* is small car, a kind of collective taxi or minibus.

# Chapter 15

# Christmas in the Village

It was the beginning of December. One day, when Renate and I were out in the car, some young people we didn't know approached us.

"When is the Christmas service this year?" they asked.

"On the nineteenth," Renate replied readily.

As we went on our way I asked Renate why they would want to know since they didn't belong to our church.

"We always get a lot of visitors from across the whole area," she explained. "The Christmas service is a big event for everybody and a good opportunity for us to tell many people the Christmas message."

"And why don't we celebrate it on the 24th or the 25th, like everyone else in the world?"

"There are only a few congregations in this area and they are mostly very small. Some of them have no staff of their own to lead the services. This means you can't celebrate Christmas everywhere on the same day. Anyway, as the congregations want to visit one another, everyone agrees on a date ahead of time. We will also go to the different Christmas services. You'll see."

Christmas in the villages of southern Sumatra is a community event. Our Western family celebration is an odd concept there because families include the extended family, which can mean half the village.

On the morning of the agreed date, the children trooped into the jungle to get materials for the Christmas tree. They returned with lots of greenery to use to create the branches. Someone had brought a banana plant log and someone else some bamboo. The bamboo was split into thin lattices and poked into the banana log and some moss-like greenery was wrapped around the lattices. The "Christmas tree" was beginning to take shape – you could have been forgiven for thinking it was a real tree. Candle holders made of round bamboo pieces were placed on the ends of the bamboo sticks jutting out of the greenery. I had made a few stars out of gold paper to hang on the tree. The tree, as well as the inside of the church, was decorated with colourful crepe paper streamers. I was certainly looking forward to the meeting in the evening!

The leaders met before the service to go over the last-minute details. The evening was divided into three sections: first the service, then some greetings and speeches and lastly an open programme where everyone had the opportunity to contribute. The village head and the village *imam* had both been invited to give a greeting. As many people were expected, we had to get permission from the police for the celebration. Two policemen charged with maintaining order, turned up.

The service was due to start at 7 pm but it was nearly 7.30 when the service finally began. Even then not all guests from outside the village had arrived. The planks on the front wall of the church had been removed so that those outside could easily see what was happening inside the building. The young people sat on the grassy slope outside the church to watch while the little children sat on a mat next to the Christmas tree. Our youth group and a guest group each sang a song, and the candles on the tree were lit while the congregation sang "Silent night". The Christmas story was read and followed by a sermon, both in Indonesian. The women's choir sang and the service itself drew to a close.

Next the Chair of the Christmas committee gave a short speech, apologising for anything that might go wrong during the celebrations. This is typical in Indonesia. The village head and the leader of the congregation then gave formal greetings. In between the different greetings and speeches we enjoyed listening to a number of songs.

Finally, the long-awaited open programme of songs, dances and other creative pieces began. Sweet tea and cookies were served throughout the programme. Our youth group and a guest group both sang and other visitors contributed to the entertainment. The last item was a short play, performed by the young people, about family problems and was straight out of ordinary life. Everyone had been waiting for it and it was the highlight of the evening. Then, with hearty greetings in Indonesian for Christmas and the New Year, the party came to an end and the guests took their leave. It was nearly midnight when I got home.

The next morning we got up at dawn, just before 6 am, as usual. It was a day for visiting all the Christian families. We had to hurry as the visits were to begin at our home at 8 o'clock. We quickly prepared plates of biscuits and drinks, pushed the living room furniture to one side and spread out mats. On the dot of 8 o'clock the pastor, elders and other staff members of the church were at our door. We greeted each other cheerfully and chatted about the previous evening. We all agreed that it had been a successful celebration. We sang some Christmas songs together and prayed for the challenge of the day and of the New Year that was before us.

It was our plan to visit all the members of the congregation in their homes and to leave them with a blessing as we sang and prayed for them. As there were about 40 Christian families in the congregation, we decided to split into two groups with one group visiting the homes along the road going in the direction of the coast, and the other group visiting the homes in the opposite direction and around the village square.

The mats were already spread out for us to sit on as people were expecting us. In each home we chatted about the year that was ending, sang a carol, read a portion of Scripture and prayed for the family. They served us with all sorts of snacks – roasted peanuts or fried bananas, sweet tea or squash. Around lunchtime we were even served chicken and rice. We didn't stay long in any house as we were expected at the next one. The make-up of our group changed constantly as more adults and young people joined our party in order to visit their neighbours. Others stayed longer in a particular home because the people there were part of their family. Eventually we reached the last house. It was already half past three when I walked across the village square towards my home.

"Come in to us!" people called out to me from their homes. I couldn't bring myself to walk by so I visited a few more families. It was nearly five o'clock when I finally reached home, tired but satisfied and greeted excitedly by our dogs.

What a way to celebrate Christmas!

# Chapter 16

# Workshop in Irian Jaya

In the mail which Renate and Ursula had brought with them was a letter from our mission headquarters in Germany. Among other things it conveyed the news that a large donation had been given for me and would become available in the course of the following month. Naturally, I was very happy but wondered how I should use the money as I had everything I needed at that particular time.

Ursula had had a lot of experience in language research and Bible trans-lation in Indonesia, and as I talked with her about my plans, she gave me some good advice.

"You should start putting the Serawai data you have collected onto index cards. That will help you put the material in order so you can easily find what you need when you come to do language analysis." I also talked with her about my findings in relation to phonetics[10], especially concerning those sounds that create a difference in meaning in words and would therefore need special attention when it came to developing the language's orthogra-phy[11]. I could see that I was on the right track; but that I needed to collect more data and more examples so decided I would concentrate on that.

A few days later I received a letter from the mission leaders in Batu with an invitation to a two-month workshop on lexicography in Irian Jaya, the western part of New Guinea, at the eastern end of Indonesia, about 3000 kilometres away. The leader suggested that I should seriously consider tak-ing part.

"Lexicography – that's about the production of a dictionary, isn't it?"

"It certainly is," Ursula confirmed.

"But I have not reached that stage yet," I said. "Surely, I am still right at the beginning of language research. I have to determine the spelling first."

"That's true. But you would learn a whole lot there for which you would be grateful later on. Maybe you would even get informal help in relation to the orthography. If you can afford it, I would very much advise you to go."

---

[10]  *Phonetics* is a part of phonology (the study of sound).

[11]  *Orthography* is the spelling of a language's words.

Well, I had just received that big gift. God knew of the workshop long before and had put it on someone's heart to make a donation so that I would have the money available on time. How wonderfully God had looked after everything!

At the beginning of the workshop I spoke with the leading professor about my situation.

"Why don't you write a phonemic outline of the Serawai language while you are here," he suggested. "I will gladly be of assistance if you would like any help."

Everything was falling into place.

Meiril, a young man from Serawai, who had just completed Bible school in Batu, was in Irian Jaya at the time to gain practical ministry experience. Not only was he in Irian Jaya, he was in Abepura, the town I was in. We met up twice a week and he proved an invaluable source of information. It meant I returned to Sumatra with a well thought-through orthography. An important milestone had been reached.

# Chapter 17

# My Translation Helper Sida

I needed a language assistant and Sida, who lived just two houses away, came to mind. Having completed six years primary school she moved to Manna, where she stayed with an uncle, to continue her education. When her uncle demanded that she convert to Islam, she decided to drop out of school and return to her mother in the village. Her father had already been dead a long time. When she started to help me she was in her early twenties and appeared to be stable and mature. At church she was deeply involved in both the children's church and in the children's club. I was able to work well with her and was glad that she didn't always just say "yes", but corrected me and even put forward different opinions.

Having set up the spelling patterns of the language, I wanted to begin translating the New Testament. I chose a number of different stories from the Gospels which, I hoped, would be published later on in a book outlining Jesus' life. When I told Sida about this idea, she hesitated.

"I can't do that," she said. I tried to encourage her and suggested she should at least give it a try. "No," she responded, "it's too difficult for me. This is God's Word. You can't make mistakes."

I was pleased that she understood the responsibilities of a translator and that it was a task that shouldn't be tackled lightly. "Once something is translated, it doesn't mean it is set in stone. It will be revised and corrected, until we feel that it really reflects the meaning of the text. You'll see," I said as I sought to encourage her.

I was also unsure about my own capabilities as a translator. After all, it was five years since I had done the course at SIL[12] and had learnt about translation methods. Recently, I had come across a new book on this topic which clearly described different translation principles. To revise what I had learnt, I worked through that book chapter by chapter.

Some time earlier the Indonesian Bible Society had brought out a pamphlet in the Serawai language telling the story of the creation and fall. It had come together during a workshop with local translators. Unfortunately, there was a serious spelling error in that a particular consonant had been written as

---

[12] *SIL* stands for *Summer Institute of Linguistics* and is a sister organisation of the *Wycliffe Bible Translators*.

a vowel, and there were other major translation errors which had not been picked up during the short workshop. Using this pamphlet we tried to put into practice the different translation principles. Sida experienced firsthand how a sentence that had previously been translated could be rejected and revised. We grappled with the translation, not only to fully grasp the meaning of God's Word but also to express it in her language in a natural and fluent way. Taking into account different aspects of the translation principles, we revised this tract together several times. Little by little Sida began to get the hang of it and became a valuable co-worker. This was important as only an indigenous speaker can best judge what a sentence should sound like.

A few years later, after we had translated half of the New Testament, Sida had a crisis and told me she wanted to quit translating. I was shocked. I couldn't imagine working without her. By then she had so much experience and we had a really good working relationship. It would take a long time to train such another good translation helper.

"The work is too hard and the responsibility too big," was her short reply when I asked her why.

She didn't tell me the real reason, but on no account did I want to lose her. I knew her well enough to know that once she had made up her mind about something, she rarely changed it.

"Lord, I need wisdom," I prayed silently.

"You know, Sida," I said, "translating the Bible is God's work and I know it is not an easy task. You must remember that you are not working for me, but for Him, even though I pay you. I can't force you do to this work, but equally I can't simply release you from it either. You have to get the permission to quit from God. Why don't you take time to pray and ask God about it?"

We stopped our work for the day and after a prayer I let her go home.

That night I slept little. I kept asking myself if I had handled it right. Over the past weeks, Sida and I had often had big arguments whilst translating. I had the impression that she was not really with it and was doing her work half-heartedly. Had it become too stressful for her? Was it my fault? I asked God for greater sensitivity and asked Him to show us how the work should continue. I especially asked Him to meet with Sida and give her a new perspective. We needed Him and His leading. We couldn't do this work on our own.

I was relieved when Sida turned up next morning.

"*Ibu*[13]," she said, "I'll carry on."

I breathed a sigh of relief and thanked God for working it out.

---

[13] *Ibu* means mother and is the respectful way to address a woman.

# Chapter 18

# A New Word

"What on earth is that?"

I was in the middle of cleaning my room when I lifted my typewriter case and discovered something black underneath. I thought it might be a scorpion all curled up and taking its midday nap, but I wasn't sure. What should I do with it? I had had no experience with scorpions and didn't know how they reacted. I was not sure what to do and Renate had gone shopping in Manna. Then I remembered that a short while earlier some patients had arrived and were waiting for Renate to return. I was just about to go and get them when I realised that I didn't know what to tell them.

"What is 'scorpion' in the Serawai language?" I wondered.

I didn't know the word, and I didn't even know it in Indonesian, but I did have an Indonesian dictionary. The dictionary was on the lowest shelf of the bookcase behind the scorpion. Carefully, so as not to disturb the creature, I took the dictionary from the shelf. Against the word "scorpion" I read the words *"kala jengking"*. I tried to remember them, work out what to say and went to the people waiting at the front of the house.

"Could you help me?" I asked, after a short greeting. "I have a *kala jengking* in my room." The men looked at me blankly.

"What's the problem?"

"A *kala jengking*. Could you help me remove it from my room?"

These Serawai men knew as little Indonesian as I did and, apparently, they didn't understand the word for scorpion. But they were prepared to stand by me in the battle against any dangerous animal, so I simply asked them to come with me and to see it for themselves. When we reached the back door, I gave them some sticks to equip them for the battle. I sensed their curiosity mounting as we reached my room, but the scorpion had gone. Where was it? I scanned the floor. Had it escaped under the bookcase, or hidden itself somewhere else?

I lifted up the typewriter case again and, sure enough, there it was! Sensing the threat, it raised itself up to its full height and turned towards us, ready for the attack. It appeared to be waiting, ready to put up a fight with any attacker. It was an imposing animal, its pincers nearly 15 cm apart. The tail with its poisonous dart was curled up and hanging over, ready to strike. I had never seen anything like it before.

With one big whack one of the men stunned the scorpion. "That is a *kalau*," they informed me and walked away, laughing.

# Chapter 19

# Not for Fearful Souls

I was lying on my bed, having my lunchtime rest and reading a book. I liked to read lying down as sometimes it helped me fall asleep. On the wicker armchair diagonally opposite, right next to the door that led outside, our cat was also having his siesta.

I heard him leap softly off the chair. I peered over the edge of my book and saw him coming towards me, presumably for a cuddle. But he didn't even look at me. Something under my bed had captured his full attention. He was beginning to tense up. Slowly he crept closer. About a metre from my bed he stopped, poised to leap. Maybe, I thought, he had found a spider or some other insect, and I returned to my book.

Then I heard a hiss coming from the direction of the wall under the top end of my bed. The cat jumped aside. I caught a glimpse of something dark disappearing under the bookcase opposite. The cat leapt after it and half a metre in front of the bookcase crouched down low, keeping the creature in sight.

"That wasn't a rat," the thought crossed my mind. I took my torch and shone it under the bookcase. There I discovered, curled up against the wall, a fairly big, dark snake. The cat kept guard while I went to fetch Renate. When we returned, the cat had not moved from his post in front of the bookcase which had a curtain hanging in front of it. I shone my torch underneath and asked Renate if she could see the snake. All she saw was the last few centimetres of tail disappearing behind the shelf. As the shelf did not have a back, it seemed the snake must have crawled into it from behind, in order to hide.

I removed the curtain from the front of the bookcase but we found nothing suspicious. Using a stick I tried to move various objects from the bookcase onto the floor. Bravely, Renate grabbed the bookcase at the side and pulled it away from the wall but we still could not see anything. We kept looking and carefully, slowly, bit by bit, removed my things from the bookcase. The snake seemed to have disappeared into thin air. But we knew it must be there in the bookcase somewhere. After all, we'd seen it crawl into it!

"Look," Renate said suddenly. "Isn't that a bit of its tail?"

There was a black cassette deck in the corner of the shelf. Above it there was a space of about five centimetres. The snake had squeezed itself into that tiny space and had curled itself up.

"Now what do we do?"

"No idea. Let's get someone from the village."

I went to the front of the house and looked down into the village but couldn't see anyone. It was early afternoon and most people were on their fields or having a siesta. Where could I go to get help? Then I saw Nenek Em, the mother of my translation helper Sida, behind my neighbour's house.

"Ui, *Nenek*[14]! Can you help us?" I called to her.

The neighbour also came round the corner. "What's the matter?"

"There's a snake in my bedroom."

We felt sure that these two experienced local people would have no problem dealing with the snake. We showed them where the snake was hiding, still curled up in the same place.

"It's best to catch it with a looped string," our neighbour said.

I couldn't for the life of me imagine how that would work.

"Wouldn't it be better if one of us pushes it out of its hiding place from one end and someone else catches it when it comes out the other end?" I suggested.

They agreed to try that.

The neighbour pushed the snake out of its hiding place with a stick, and Nenek Em, armed with a broom handle, waited on the other side. At first the snake did not move, but then it came out of its dark corner and dropped to the floor. Too quick for Nenek Em to deal with, it glided to the wall and found safety under the table and chair. From there it slithered along the wall, back under the bed and under the wardrobe at the foot of the bed. Next to the wardrobe was the door into the trainee student's room. This door couldn't be opened from my room as there was a big cupboard full of medicine for the clinic on the other side, but there was a gap of about three centimetres under the door through which the snake disappeared.

"Now it is in the next room!" I shouted, horrified.

"Let's go there, then," someone suggested pragmatically.

All four of us searched the room, but found nothing.

Both of our helpers were getting tired and sat down in the living room.

"It has to be here." Renate was not giving up easily. "Come on, Hildegard, let's keep looking."

---

[14] *Nenek* is the polite way of addressing an older lady and means 'grandmother'.

"Maybe it's behind the cupboard." I shone my light there, but couldn't see anything.

"Shine behind there again," Renate suggested. "I'll try to move it just a bit."

When Renate leant against the cupboard with all her strength, it moved a little, and I saw the snake, about half way up and right next to Renate's hands.

"We've found it. Please, come and help us," we shouted to our helpers.

We discussed the plan of action. The neighbour fetched a long bamboo stick and cut one end into a sharp two-pronged fork. One of us poked the snake, which was still behind the cupboard, with this stick so that it fell to the floor. It slithered under the bed which was next to the cupboard. The neighbour kept prodding it with the prongs of his bamboo stick until it stopped writhing.

"It was looking for a place to lay eggs," he said as he dragged the snake from under the bed. It was about a metre and a half. "The eggs are all squashed."

Renate and I were relieved and glad that we had not given up. We certainly didn't want a snake's nest in our house! In the evening we told our story to the grandmothers who had come to visit us. The next morning one of them greeted me then asked, "Did you check under all the cupboards last night before going to bed to see if there were any more snakes?"

"No," I replied, slightly bemused. "Should I have done that?"

"I would have done," she said. "Are you not afraid that there might be another snake?"

Her words haunted me for a while afterwards.

"No," I decided. "If I start checking all corners for fear of more snakes, how can I live here? If I start doing that, I might as well pack up and go home now."

With that I decided against fear and continued to sleep peacefully at night knowing that God was watching over me.

# Chapter 20

# Which Language to Use?

Renate had been shopping in Manna. As soon as the village children heard her car approaching, they ran out to meet her, ready to help carry the shopping up the slope to our house. The children shared out the bags of groceries, fruit and vegetables between them so that they all had something to carry. Almost in a procession, they followed each other up the slope. When they dropped off the bags at the house, each one was rewarded with a sweet.

The last child was just getting her sweet as Renate reached the last of the steps.

"Any news from Manna?" I called to her.

"I bumped into our *camat*[15] and his wife," she said. "He's being transferred to a new post. His wife is really sad to be moving away."

"Yes, she always enjoyed our visits. Where are they moving to?"

"To Padang Guci[16]. I promised her we would visit her there one day. The official handover is next Wednesday. They've invited us to attend."

"That's unusual, isn't it? Who else is invited?" I asked.

"All the village heads in our district. We mustn't refuse the invitation. They would be very disappointed if we did."

I was reminded of the time I had gone to the district office during my first visit to southern Sumatra. Renate, who had had to go there to register, had taken me on the back of her motorbike. The offices were about 20 kilometres upriver and as the bridge was not passable we had had to make a detour via the district town of Manna. At that time the road from Manna had not been tarred and, having fallen off the bike at one mud hole and badly burned my calf on the hot exhaust pipe, I got off whenever we approached a mud hole. I remembered my distinct impression that the officials at the district office were astonished to see two white ladies arriving on a Honda 100. They were more used to seeing ladies on mopeds or scooters or riding side-saddle on the back of a motorbike driven by a man.

---

[15] *Camat* is a sub-district leader.

[16] *Padang Guci* is a sub-district about 50 kilometres further south.

61

On that occasion, the *camat* had greeted us in person and after the official business had sent us to see his wife in the house next door. She treated us as very special guests and we spent a lovely time with her. Coming from another island, she herself felt like a stranger and obviously welcomed our visit as a change to her monotonous daily routine. After that we visited her from time to time, even without the excuse of an official errand.

Yes, even though we were not really keen on those official receptions, we did not want to disappoint the hosts.

Accompanied by the village heads of our own and the neighbouring village, we set out at 8.30 on the Wednesday morning. When we arrived, we found that chairs had been set up on a covered terrace and that right at the front were some rattan armchairs. As honoured guests we were taken to sit in these more comfortable seats. Slowly the remaining seats began to fill up.

Just after 10 o'clock the *bupati*[17] who was presiding over the official handover, the *camat* and his successor, came out of the office, surprisingly on time.

The outgoing *camat* greeted everyone, then the *bupati* conducted the official handover to the new *camat* and finally addressed the village heads. Normally such official business was conducted in Indonesian, the national language, according to the government motto of "One country, one language, one nation". The *bupati*, who had only been district director in Manna for one or two years, came originally from this area and understood the mentality of the Serawai people. He knew that these men, even if they were village heads, had only a limited grasp of the Indonesian language. So he addressed them in their mother tongue – the Serawai language. In that way he gained their full attention and was successfully able to pass on the latest government programmes.

I understood very little of what was said, but one thing I did understand: if you want to motivate people and if you want to reach their hearts, you have to speak to them in a language they understand. If the district director could use the local language to explain the government's plans to the village heads, so that they could support and implement those plans in their villages, how much more should we be using the local language in our church services to explain a much more important plan than any government plan – God's plan for humanity and how life can be significant even into eternity.

---

[17] *Bupati* is a district director.

# Chapter 21

# Brief Encounters

I had noticed that small talk in Indonesian differed from that in German. In Germany, for example, if you are travelling, you might chat to fellow travellers about the weather. On the whole the conversation, at least at first, would remain fairly anonymous. In Indonesia, it seemed to me that personal questions come up rather quickly. Questions such as "What is your name?" "Where do you live?" "How old are you?" are seen as conversation starters. When I realised this, I tried to accept it and not to be irritated by it. I worked out some suitable coping strategies and, as a result, sometimes ended up having very interesting and quite funny conversations. Here are just a few examples.

One day at the beach in Bengkulu someone started a conversation with me.

"What is your name?" he asked.

"My name is Hildegard," I replied.

"Where are you from?"

"From Germany."

"Where do you live?"

"I live in the south."

"How old are you?"

"Older than you think. I am really already over thirty." That was not a lie, even if a slight understatement.

"Really? You seem much younger." Smiling, I nodded back.

"How many children do you have?"

"None. I am not married."

"Well, then you could marry an Indonesian?"

"Possibly."

"What are you doing here?"

"I work for the church."

"Which one, Catholic or Protestant?"

"The Protestant Church."

"What is actually the difference?"

And so we found ourselves in the middle of a conversation about the Christian faith.

On one occasion in the waiting room at the doctor's, I got chatting to a young man. The conversation began in a similar way. When I told him that I worked for the church he said, "I am a Muslim. We believe in God. And you?"

"We Christians also believe in God. We believe that Jesus Christ is also God and we believe in the Holy Spirit, through whom God works in this world."

We chatted a bit longer about our faith in God.

Then he said, "Muslims pray five times a day. Do you pray?"

"Yes, of course we also pray. We pray together during church services or alone at home. We thank Him for everything good and also bring Him our requests."

"Before we Muslims pray, we first wash our hands and our face. What about you?"

"We Christians cleanse ourselves not on the outside, but on the inside. We ask God for forgiveness for our sins, because Jesus has carried the guilt of our sins on the cross."

"We Muslims fast at Ramadan from sunrise to sunset. Do you fast?"

"Yes, Christians also fast sometimes. But it is not prescribed, as it is for you. We choose to fast to have more time to pray and to concentrate better as we do so."

That was where the conversation ended as he was called into the doctor's surgery.

Another time, I was waiting at the airport in Bengkulu to pick up a guest. I had managed to find somewhere to sit, and a young man, I guess mid to late twenties, sat down next to me. He immediately started up a conversation with the usual questions. I was not in the best of moods that day and would much rather have had some peace and quiet, so only answered him grudgingly, without turning towards him. He didn't seem to notice, which really irritated me, and continued to ask questions. When he found out that I was not married, he said happily, "Great! Then you can marry an Indonesian. Would you do that?"

"No, I don't really want to," was my curt answer. That, perhaps, was not entirely honest, but I was hoping he would finally realise that I was not interested in a conversation right then. Perhaps that hadn't been such a good answer after all because he turned to me indignantly. "What's wrong with us Indonesian men?"

I tried to appease him and explained that cultural differences could create all sorts of problems in a marriage. I was thankful when I finally spotted my guest and our conversation was over.

On another occasion, when I had travelled to a different province to take part in a seminar, I went, as usual, to register with the police. A policeman went through the usual questions. When he found out that I was not married, he immediately perked up, "You could marry an Indonesian. You could do that, couldn't you?"

I remembered the disastrous conversation at the airport and decided to answer more positively. "Yes, I could," I said. I was hoping that he wouldn't make a proposal there and then. In my dreams ...

"What about me? I am still single," he offered readily.

The other policemen standing around laughed. How was I to get out of this one without hurting anyone's feelings?

Quick as a flash I replied, "Can you speak German so that you can talk to my parents? Because they don't speak any English."

"No," he answered, disappointed. "I could just about manage English. But German? Perhaps it wouldn't work out between us after all."

# Chapter 22

# Driving Licence

"Could you exchange my international driving licence for an Indonesian one?" My international driving licence was about to run out and I needed a new one.

The police officer in Manna answered in the negative. I looked at him, somewhat at a loss.

"You could take a driving test. Then you would get a driving licence," he suggested.

"What would I need for that?"

He checked in his files. "We would need a copy of your passport, ID card and the immigration card, then your blood type and two passport photos."

"And where can I register for the test?"

"We do driving tests every Saturday morning, starting at 8 o'clock with the written test. You don't have to register. You just turn up."

"What happens during a test?"

"There is a written multiple choice test, an oral test about traffic signs and a driving test," he explained helpfully.

"Do you have a Highway Code, or something that describes and explains the traffic rules and signs?"

"No, we don't."

"Where can I get hold of something like that? I want to come to the test prepared."

"I don't know."

"Could I take my motorbike test at the same time?"

"Yes, of course that is possible."

"And what would it all cost?" He named the price.

When I was in Java, I had heard that you could get your driving licence without a test if you paid a little more, but the policeman here didn't hint at that possibility.

I couldn't find a Highway Code or anything like it anywhere but, on the whole, the road signs were the same as the ones in Germany, so I relied on my knowledge of those.

Very early the following Saturday morning, I left for Manna. The main road in the town centre was blocked off, with a no through sign for motorbikes "unless wearing a helmet". Hardly any motorcyclists ever wore a helmet and it seemed the authorities wanted to insist that they should.

I arrived at the police station at 8 am and parked my car in the big car park where there was just one other car, and went to the reception.

"I want to take the driving test," I told the police officer on duty. "Where do I have to go?" He pointed the way to the relevant room.

I filled in the application form and put the required photocopies with it. Then a policeman took me to the next room. About fifteen young people were already working on their written test. The officer in charge handed me a question paper, several pages long. I soon became engrossed in it. The multiple choice questions were quite interesting, "What should you do if you have caused an accident? Stop, drive away or drive to the next police station?" "What should you do if the road is full of potholes? Drive straight over, or zigzag around the holes?" "What different lights does a vehicle have, and what do the colours of the lights mean?" "If you borrow a friend's motorbike, is it enough to take his driving licence or do you need your own?"

Sometimes I read a question twice, to make sure I hadn't misread it. When I had finished I handed in my question paper and left the room and waited outside with the other test participants.

About half an hour later we were called up one by one. About half of the participants hadn't passed the written test. I had, and together with seven others I was taken to another room where a policeman was standing by a wall on which various traffic signs were displayed. We all sat down on a bench in front of the wall. The policeman pointed to a traffic sign and asked the first person what it meant. Then he pointed to another sign. The next person was questioned about the same signs. The candidate's answers were very interesting. The "No through way" sign for motorbikes was taken to mean "This is where you have to wear a helmet", and a shrug of the shoulders answered the question relating to the "Give way" sign.

I watched the policeman carefully. He made no comment and his facial expression gave nothing away. The "Give way" sign kept being indicated, and the fourth candidate came up with the explanation, "It is a T-junction." This same answer was repeated by each of the other candidates as it seemed no-one could think of a better explanation. And then it was my turn. The policeman asked me about the same traffic signs plus a few more, and I tried to explain in Indonesian what they meant.

When we had finished, the policeman spoke for the first time, and turned to me personally. "On the whole that was all correct, although you didn't quite get some of the technical terms, but the content was correct." To the others he said, "The rest of you can try again next week." I felt sorry for the man who had been questioned immediately before me as he had actually appeared to know quite a lot.

"You can do your practical test now," the policeman told me. "Where is your car?"

I went with the policeman to the car park at the front of the building. There, a motorcyclist was trying to ride a figure of eight around some wooden blocks that had been set up. The blocks were quite close together, and he failed to do it. He didn't manage on his second attempt either and was invited to try again the next week.

The policeman took a few of the wooden blocks and set them up to the right and left of my car. "Now drive out of this parking space to the right, and then reverse park back into the same space."

I sat down at the wheel, turned down the window and drove out, then reversed in without knocking any of the blocks over.

"Now do it again, but to the left."

Nothing was easier than that.

"Now do it again, but reverse with only the help of your mirrors." That time I didn't drive out as far and kept the wheel in place. That way I could reverse back in without having to steer – just drive out and straight back in. The policeman was satisfied with my performance. He had already seen me drive around in the car for the best part of a year and knew that I was not a bad driver. He could see that I knew how to reverse park even though there was little need to reverse park in this town where there were so few cars.

I was happy when he said, "You can collect your driving licence at the office."

I decided to leave getting the motorbike licence that day, planning to practise a bit more.

Six months later, when our road was in too bad a shape for the car, I remembered I needed a driving licence for the motorbike, so one Saturday morning, around 9 o'clock, I turned up at the police station.

"Why are you late? We started at 8 o'clock," they chided me.

"But I was told I only had to take the practical part of the test as I have already passed the written and oral parts," I replied.

"Ah, that is different. Wait a moment. I just have to find the documents." With that the policeman disappeared.

About 15 minutes later he returned. "When did you do the test?" he asked.

"About six months ago."

He came back after another ten minutes.

"I am very sorry, but unfortunately we can't find the documents. You will have to repeat the written test." He seemed somewhat crestfallen.

"That's ok," I reassured him.

With a different policeman I went to the room next door. There was no-one else there. He read the first question out loud to me and then said, "Now tick B."

"Thank you. But I think I can do this by myself."

"As you wish," he said, handing me the question paper.

I knew the questions and worked through them quickly. Then I handed the question paper back to the policeman. He marked it and found one mistake.

"It is perhaps better if it is not all correct," he commented.

We went back to the office. The staff there were obviously feeling sorry for me having to redo the written test and let me skip the practical motorcycling test. I didn't mind and received the motorcycle licence there and then. I thanked them and went out to Pak John who was waiting for me with the motorbike, a Honda 100. He started the engine and I sat myself side saddle on the passenger seat behind him. I waved cheerfully to the policemen as we drove off. I now had my motorbike licence – Pak John actually didn't have one!

# Chapter 23

# Broken Bones

It was the dry season. There had been no rain for two weeks and our water butts and basins were empty. As we didn't have a well we had to carry our water in buckets from the public spring which was down a steep, narrow path behind our house. The spring was lined with concrete and the low walls created a natural basin for the water. Several families went there to wash.

That morning the sky was heavy and the air close. We were just finishing our breakfast when I heard a distant rushing sound and noticed the first dark rain spots on the cement paving around our house.

Renate and I were overjoyed as the rain got stronger and stronger and turned into a real downpour. It ran off the roof into our drums which were soon full to the brim and beginning to overflow.

"Hildegard, get the buckets. Let's fill up the basins in the bathrooms."

Again and again, we filled up our buckets and carried them to our two bathrooms. It felt wonderful to see so much clear water. We hurried back and forth, taking care not to slip on the damp cement floor which sloped a little towards the open drain around our house, making it easier for the rain water to drain away.

When we had filled the basins, Renate went round the corner to pour a couple of buckets of water over the cement floor there. It needed it, because the chickens that ran around freely had left their dirt behind. We drew more and more water out of the overflowing drums. It was fun to be able to be so wasteful with water for once. I decided to draw one last bucketful. And then it happened. One wrong step and I slipped. The next thing I knew I was lying helplessly in the open drain. Just at that moment Renate came round the corner again.

"What ever are you doing?"

"Can't you see?"

Renate helped me to my feet, took me to my room and helped me take off my wet clothes. My arm hurt with every move I made.

I had barely dressed when there was a knock at my door. It was Nenek Em, Sida's mother.

"I hear you fell and hurt yourself."

As I was telling her what had happened, Renate came in with a bandage so that I could put my arm in a sling. But the pain did not go away. In actual fact, it was getting worse.

"I think it's broken. What do we do now?"

"We need to get it x-rayed really," Renate said. "Let me finish up at the clinic and then we'll drive to Bengkulu."

Because of the rain, there were only a few patients that morning and Renate was able to close the clinic early. We quickly ate a few mouthfuls of rice and left at about 11 o'clock.

It was just after 2 o'clock when we arrived at the hospital where we were told that the radiologist had gone home and we would have to return the next day. It was just as well we had taken overnight things with us.

The next day I returned to the village with my arm in plaster. No-one in the village had ever seen anything like it before.

"That's like concrete," the women exclaimed when they touched it.

"How are you going to eat?" one of them asked.

"What do you mean?"

"You know, how are you going to eat? Your hand doesn't even reach your mouth."

She was quite right. My right arm was fixed at a right angle and I couldn't get my hand to my mouth. Here in the village people ate with their right hands. As the left hand was only used for "dirty business", it would be unheard of to eat using that hand. I told her I would manage with a spoon. She seemed reassured that I was not going to go hungry.

About two weeks later my neighbours were having a small party and I was invited for lunch. The men sat in a circle in the front room and were served food by the young lads. The women were busy dishing out the food at the back of the house. They invited me to join them and I sat alone in the passage between the kitchen and front room and was served my food there.

"Would you like a spoon?" they asked me.

"No thank you," I replied. "I think I'll be OK."

I was aware that what I was about to do would be a challenge to the people. I was going to eat with my left hand. I had no problem with that. After all, I didn't use it for "dirty business" but the people didn't know that. One of the young men watching me eat looked horrified and about to be sick. Perhaps I really had gone too far!

When I had finished eating, I stayed where I was. One woman asked me, "Why aren't you leaving?" I looked a little surprised.

The other women laughed. "She's our neighbour," the hostess explained. It was customary, at a feast, to get up and leave straight away after finishing your food to make space for other guests.

I found it all quite bizarre, though in a way amusing. Without my sense of humour, it would have been so much harder to get on in that culture, so alien to my own.

# Chapter 24

# Like a Monkey in a Zoo

Renate was very excited. "I have an invitation to Rigangan," she called out to me.

"The road to Kedurang is meant to be passable. If it doesn't rain, I am going there next Friday. You'll come along, won't you?" she added.

"Of course I'll come. It will give me the chance to test how different the language there really is compared to the Serawai here."

Rigangan is a village in Kedurang, an area south of Manna, where they speak Pasemah. I had heard that on the whole it was the same language as Serawai, but that words didn't end in "au" but in "e". I wanted to check that out.

I asked Renate how she had this contact.

"Ibu Situmpul, the older Batak lady who comes to the service on the oil palm plantation," she said, "tells me her son is married there. He is the only Christian in the village. As the lady has not seen her grandson for a long time, we will give her a lift and that gives us a good excuse to visit, plus she knows where the house is. Although the young family is living with the wife's parents, we will be well received as we are bringing the grandma. They have a big house. The young man earns money by repairing radios and other electrical items in the village."

"In that case I might take my radio-tape player for him to look at. Perhaps he can work out why the cassette deck doesn't work any more."

Renate always liked to take Indonesians with her on visits, especially men who were familiar with local customs, spoke the local dialect and were able to converse with the men about matters of faith. She had hoped that Pak Kornelius, nicknamed Pak Kor, the pastor in our village of Napal Melintang, could come with us. Unfortunately he was not free, so on Friday afternoon, after closing the clinic, we set off, accompanied only by the grandparents and our trainee student.

As usual, Renate took some medicines with her. No matter where she went, people brought the sick to her and asked her for help. She didn't want to disappoint them.

I had prepared a word list for my language studies and also took my radio-tape player and a *Gospel Recordings*[18] tape in Pasemah which explained the story of salvation from creation, the fall, Abraham and David, the birth of Jesus and His work, to His death and resurrection.

We picked up the Batak lady and her husband and on the way through Manna stopped at the market to buy some rice, noodles, vegetables and two chickens. For me, this was the first time to visit another village where we would stay overnight. The path from the coastal road into the fertile Kedurang valley was not tarmacked. We drove past extensive rice fields. The ground was not the red clay we had near Napal Melintang, but was sandier and this meant we didn't have to worry about getting stuck in large mud holes. These could be a concern for although our vehicle was a four-wheel drive, it was not a Jeep and was quite low. There were a few critical places, but we managed to get through with no major difficulties. It was already late afternoon when we reached the village.

"We have to turn off over there," the grandfather said. "Go past that sports field and the house is right behind it."

The village youth were playing a game of volleyball on the sports field and there were quite a few spectators. Because of the road conditions, we drove past them at walking speed. When the young people saw our car with a white woman driving it and another in the passenger seat, they forgot about the game. They had never seen anything like it before! They all followed us shouting and calling us "Long nose".

Soon afterwards we stopped in front of a large house. It was not built on pillars like the traditional houses, but the lower half, which was of red brick, was built at ground level and had a cement floor. The young man was at home. He greeted us and invited us in.

We unloaded the things we had brought with us and carried them into a large room in the house. At the far end of the room there was a work bench with electrical items on it. In front of the bench there was a small sitting corner with wicker chairs, where we sat down. A crowd of children and young people pushed into the room but kept a distance of one or two metres, as if an invisible barrier was stretched across the room. Of course not everyone could get into the room and there were others crowding around the windows to stare at us. The lady of the house brought us something to drink and we chatted about trivial things. The spectators were fascinated and, quiet as mice, they watched our every move, determined not to miss any part of our

---

[18] *Gospel Recordings* is an organisation that produces evangelistic tapes in different languages.

74

conversation. I felt like a monkey in a zoo or as though I was the lead role in a movie in which I didn't know the script. The only thing to do was to go along with it...

After a while I began to notice that people were leaving. The sun had gone down and most were returning to their homes to wash before darkness fell and it was time for them to eat with their families.

When we were almost alone, Renate said, "This would be a good opportunity for us to wash at the well next to the house, before it is totally dark." We were shown to the bedroom of the young family, where we could change. To wash at the well, we tied a cloth around us and poured water over ourselves with a jug. The cool water was very refreshing and, incredibly, we had no spectators. I felt a lot better afterwards.

The women of the house had, in the meantime, plucked and cooked the chickens we had brought, and it was not long before a tasty meal was served. Afterwards, I gave the young man my radio-tape player and he got to work on it straight away. If nothing else, it was getting a thorough clean.

"Do you have a tape, so I can try it out?"

"Yes," I answered happily and got my tape. The machine really did work again. Apparently it had just needed a good clean.

Meanwhile, the first visitors from the village were at the door. In this area it was customary to share guests, especially interesting ones like us. Grass mats were spread out in the big room for people to sit on. I got out my prepared word list and started asking about indigenous words. The men were happy to answer and I wrote down phonetically what they told me. I felt I was making good progress.

The room filled up with more and more men and a few women. Renate and I felt a little uncertain as our pastor was not with us. He was the one who usually entered into conversation with the men. We were not used to sitting in a large circle of men and chatting with them. Some of the women asked for medicine for their children and Renate helped them. Then a great idea came to me.

"I have brought a tape in your language. Do you want to listen to it?"

"Yes, we would," they replied.

"It is about stories in the Bible," I warned them because I knew they were all Muslims. "Are you really sure you want to listen to it?"

"Yes, of course we want to listen. Do put it on."

And so my tape player was put to use straight away. I had taken the pocket version of the pictures with me, and as I played a story I showed the picture for it and explained it again in Indonesian. In that way most of those

Muslims heard one Bible story after another for the first time in their lives. When the tape was finished, it was already quite late.

"Would you like to hear the other side as well?" I asked the men.

"Yes, of course we want to hear it too," was the prompt reply.

The other side of the tape dealt mainly with questions about Christian living, but we didn't get far – the batteries ran out. Unfortunately, I hadn't brought any spare ones and there were none in the house.

"Do you have any questions about what you have just heard?" I said, encouraging the men to respond.

"You are Protestants, aren't you? Martin Luther started this religion, didn't he? What actually did he protest about?" someone asked straight away.

It was a good opportunity to explain the basics of the Christian faith: that we are not able to earn our way to God through good works or with money, but that we are given it freely through Jesus, because on the cross He paid for our sin.

Then someone asked the question, "You are always talking about *Tuhan*[19] Jesus (Lord Jesus). But *Tuhan* refers to God. Do you want to say then that Jesus is God?"

All the questions that followed homed in on the central truths of the Christian faith. We were ready with our answers.

Towards midnight the men finally took their leave and we were able to go to bed. The family had made their bedroom, or rather their double bed, available to us. It was a small double bed, 1.6 metres wide at the most, which Renate and I shared with our trainee student. We were like sardines in a tin. In the narrow gangway around the bed, the young lady and her two children as well as the grandmother had settled down on mats. It was hot and sticky and there was very little ventilation, but we were tired and fell asleep quickly.

When we got up the next day, the head of the house was already on his way to the market to attend to his business. After breakfast I got the chance to finish my word list. Delighted about all the new words and all the new people we had met, I quickly got into the car, happy that this time there was no curious crowd to accompany us.

---

[19] *Tuhan* means 'lord', but is only used to refer to God.

# Chapter 25

# The Birthday Party that Almost Failed

It was Renate's birthday and at breakfast she announced that she wanted to invite the congregation to a thanksgiving service and some food. She asked Nenek Wil and Nenek Ipi, who had been staying with us overnight, to help with the cooking in the afternoon before they returned home.

"I still have to drive to Manna to do the shopping but will be back by half past four. That should be enough time, shouldn't it? Would you be able to bring green papayas for the vegetables?" The two grandmothers agreed and promised to be there on time.

There were only a few patients so Renate was able to close the clinic early. We had lunch then drove to Manna. Yanti, our trainee student, and Waril, a young man from the village, came with us. It had been raining a lot and for two weeks we had not been able to leave the village because the prolonged rain meant the clay soil had become as slippery as an ice rink and made it impossible to drive uphill. We had been literally "rained in". My birthday had come in the middle of that time but, with a lot of imagination, Renate had managed to bake me a birthday cake. We always had flour and margarine in the house and in the village she was able to buy duck eggs for the cake, the hens' eggs tending to be very small. She had decorated the cake with different coloured vitamin and iron tablets, which looked like multicoloured Smarties, but were a lot healthier!

As we drove up the hill to Bandungayu, I had to get out and pilot Renate over the worst areas where the rain had created deep ruts. In Manna we stopped at the post office to post our letters. As the post office did not then have post boxes all our incoming mail was taken to the church, so we went there to collect it. We didn't stay there long and then moved on to the market. There in the market you could buy everything you needed: fruit and vegetables, meat and fish and all sorts of loose and pre-packed groceries such as rice, noodles and coffee. You could buy washing powder, pots and pans, plates, lamps and kerosene cookers – everything was available there. Most of the sellers spread their goods out on rickety, covered wooden stands, but the village ladies who were selling their produce simply put down a plastic sheet on the floor and spread out their goods. We bought carrots, beans, cabbage and potatoes for the vegetable soup, three live chickens, onions, garlic, chillies, coriander leaves, turmeric and ginger. We bought everything we needed to restock our pantry and, finally, we discovered some wonderful mangoes and bought a good supply.

Satisfied with our purchases, we started our journey home. We were well on time. Renate was looking forward to the party and was in a happy mood. In Kelutum, where we had to turn off the tarred coastal road on to the red clay road to Napal Melintang, two men from our village were waiting. They squeezed into the back seat, happy to get a lift.

When we went round the first bend after Bandungayu we could see the valley with its extensive rice fields far below us. The whole valley is prone to flooding after days of rain, so the villages are usually built on higher ground. Slowly we drove down towards the valley, but long before we reached the hairpin bends a few men came towards us. They asked us where we were going and we told them we were going to our home in the next village.

"You won't get through," they warned us. "Our lorry has got stuck on the road. It has slipped into the ruts and there's no way a car could get past. The best thing would be to turn around and go back."

Renate and I looked at each other, at a loss as to know what to do. We were barely three kilometres from our village. "I'll take the other road," Renate decided resolutely. A few months ago a bridge had been completed about 20 kilometres further up the river, but going that way meant a detour of more than 50 kilometres and would take at least two hours.

"Why don't you walk back to the village with Yanti and take the chickens and the vegetables with you," Renate suggested. "Waril can stay with me and we will drive home via Masat."

Yanti and I got out of the vehicle, picked up the various plastic bags filled with vegetables and spices, as well as the live chickens, and started walking. Renate, meanwhile, reversed back up the hill. When we reached the next bend in the road, we saw some men sitting at the side of the road. "Are you already bringing us some food?" they joked, as we passed them with our chickens.

Further down the hill we walked past the lorry which had got stuck in the ruts. The way back to the village seemed to take forever. Our arms ached from carrying the chickens and the vegetables. It was nearly five o'clock when we reached home. Our *neneks* had already got our house key from the pastor's house and had started the preparations. Nenek Wil had opened a few coconuts with the machete and was grating the white coconut flesh ready to soak in water before squeezing it out to make delicious coconut milk for the meat sauce.

While Nenek Ipi slaughtered the chickens and drained their blood, I heated the water ready for them to be dipped in before they were plucked. Then the two women cut the chickens into small, bite-size pieces. I cleaned the vegetables and Yanti prepared the spices. After they were washed, rough salt was added to the spices which were then ground into a pulp on a stone plate, using a stone pestle.

We had a couple of kerosene cookers in the kitchen on which we cooked the vegetable stew and the papaya vegetable dish. The two ladies cooked the chicken outside on a wood fire. They set up our big wok on three large stones and lit a fire underneath it. They briefly stir-fried the spices in a bit of oil, and then added the meat. Lastly they added the coconut milk and the pot full of chicken simmered away gently. The rice was also cooked in a big pan on the fire. The papayas were cut into small strips and cooked with the chickens' giblets which had been cut up into tiny pieces. Nothing was wasted!

The meal was ready and it was getting dark when Renate finally arrived.

The neighbours and the whole of our congregation came to the celebration in the evening. Everyone sat on mats in a circle. We started with a service and afterwards masses of plates of food were passed around. Renate was happy that everything had worked out so well and everyone was glad to be joining in this pleasant get-together on her birthday.

Chapter 26

# That Really is Our Language

"Have a look and see if you can read this."

I handed Nenek Wini a piece of paper. She was sitting with Nenek Wil and Nenek Ipi on the mat in our living room. Nenek Wini, the oldest of the three ladies, was the only one of them who, during the Dutch occupation of Indonesia, had gone to school and learnt to read. When she was working in her field, she often read from her Indonesian Bible during her lunch break. She could only read very slowly but she appeared to understand most of what she read.

She took the piece of paper eagerly. It was a Bible story in the Serawai language which I had printed off my computer. I had started to read my translated texts to the ladies who came in the evenings and to talk to them about what I had written. In actual fact, they were convinced that it was not possible to write down their language. Nenek Wini looked at my note carefully. Expectantly, I noticed her lips move. A smile spread across her face and after a while she nodded.

"Good," I said. "I wonder if you could read the story to the others? Renate and I have to go off to a service."

I grabbed my torch, picked up my Bible and followed Renate out of the front door into the dark night. We returned a good two hours later. The three ladies were still sitting on the mat, weaving the baskets which they had brought with them to work on.

"Well, how was your evening?" I greeted them. I was eager to know if reading out loud worked, because the language has a few unusual sounds which don't appear in Indonesian. Even younger readers need time before being able to read Serawai fluently.

"Oh! We spent all evening laughing," they answered cheerfully.

"Was it all wrong?" I asked with consternation.

"No, it was so lovely. That really is our language, just as we speak it."

Even so, they still couldn't quite grasp that it really was possible to write down their language.

# Chapter 27

# An Unforgettable Bus Journey

"We'll be leaving in just a minute!"

Renate and I had been hearing that sentence for the last hour or so. We were on the last leg of our journey home from the yearly staff conference in Batu, East Java, and were sitting on a bus to Napal Melintang at the bus station in Bengkulu.

By that time I had been in Indonesia for five years and planned to be in Germany to spend Christmas with my parents on my first, well-earned home visit. The yearly visa extension in Indonesia was a process taking months and, unfortunately, it had still not been completed. I had hoped that on my return from Java I would finally be able to collect affirmative news from the immigration department in Jakarta here at the provincial office in Bengkulu so that I could get the visa entered into my passport and then apply for my exit re-entry visa. It was not to be.

I really didn't want to have to travel to Bengkulu again before I was due to leave some four weeks later, so I had asked an American colleague living in the town to go to the authorities and sort out the necessary formalities on my behalf. Now we were sitting on the bus, waiting to go back to our village

It was not a big bus like our German buses. In Indonesia they are built for the narrow, winding roads, and the seats are more suited to the slighter build of the Indonesian people. Most of the buses were even smaller than the one we were travelling on. It was already quite full and everyone's luggage had been loaded onto the roof and tied down. The next bus belonging to this company was also ready and waiting and beginning to fill up.

I watched the hurly-burly around us and thought back over the last few days. Suddenly I remembered that I had forgotten to give my passport to my American colleague. A quick check – there it was, still in my bag. I decided that I had no option but to go back into town.

"When is the bus leaving?" I asked.

"We'll be leaving in a minute," came the standard reply.

"Do you think you can wait another half hour? I have forgotten something and need to go off for a bit."

"No. The bus will be leaving in just a minute!"

I still couldn't see the driver.

I conferred with Renate but, in any case, I knew I had to go back into town to hand over my passport. Renate promised to wait for me at the turning where we usually got off the bus. I left my luggage with her and went on my way. My colleague was surprised to see me, and took me back to the bus station by car. I had been gone barely 20 minutes, but my bus had left.

"How annoying," I thought and asked if there was a seat on the second bus.

"Yes, but all the good seats have already been taken. There are just a few spaces in the middle."

They placed a narrow board across the gangway between the seats, creating a further seat, albeit unpadded and with no back to lean on. I had to pay the whole fare again for this makeshift seat. The journey along the tarmacked road, with its many potholes and bends, was very uncomfortable. However, we were making good progress because the buses ahead of us had already collected most of the people waiting by the side of the road.

About two hours into the journey we stopped in front of a restaurant in the small town of Tais for a break for lunch. Those who wanted could buy their lunch there. I saw immediately that the first bus was still there. As I got off the bus, I saw Renate coming out of the restaurant. I was so happy to see her and, assuming that my place next to her was still free, thought that perhaps we could continue the journey together.

"I swapped your seat with that of a man from the second bus," she said. "He can have his old seat back now." I looked at her somewhat confused.

"I am not sure he would want to swap places with me. I had to buy a ticket for a place in the gangway."

These charlatans! They had made me pay the fare twice.

At that moment the driver of the first bus came past. We asked him if there was still a space and if I could perhaps travel on his bus.

"No, the bus is really too full now. I can only offer you the space beside me on the driver's seat."

"What do you mean?" I demanded. "Won't it be too narrow for both of us and interfere with your steering?"

"It's quite a wide seat. If I edge up a bit, you'll have enough space. We often take another passenger this way." I was still a little sceptical.

"The young man can sit there," Renate interjected. "You can sit next to me."

"No," the driver objected firmly. "That's absolutely not possible."

"Why ever not?" Renate countered, but the driver ignored her.

I had a choice, either I went on the same bus as Renate and sat next to the driver, or I went back to my uncomfortable seat in the middle of the second bus. I decided on the first option.

Most passengers had got back on the bus and we got ready to leave. The driver's seat really was fairly wide. I sat down next to him, the steering wheel between us. The driver realised that I knew how to drive, even though it was unusual to have women drivers in that area. We chatted about the condition of the road, about driving and lots more. The other passengers watched us through the rearview mirror and made their comments.

Along the way we met a bus from the same company coming from the opposite direction. Both buses stopped. In the other bus a young girl was sitting next to the driver. Both drivers rolled down their windows and chatted a while, swapped some fruit and winked at each other. Then they carried on.

I could imagine that our driver was now the envy of all his colleagues. To have a white woman sitting next to him on the driver's seat had just got to be trumps!

Part 3

# Second Time around

# Chapter 28

# Leaving the Country Once More

My mother was already in the car and my father had put my suitcase in the boot and opened the gate to the road. They were about to take me to the airport. Meanwhile I was dialling the number of a prayer partner.

"What's up?" she asked.

"I can't chat for long as my parents are waiting for me in the car. But I don't know where I am going to stay overnight tomorrow when I arrive in Kuala Lumpur. And I am afraid that once I go through the controls at the airport, I may have problems."

"But why," she asked. "You know we are all praying for you!"

Yes, she was right. I didn't need to worry for God would look after me. I thanked her and put down the phone. The short conversation had encouraged me and, reassured, I joined my parents in the car.

I had a ticket from Frankfurt to Jakarta via Kuala Lumpur, Malaysia, with Malaysian Air Service (MAS). My plan was to stop off in Kuala Lumpur and go on to visit friends in Thailand. Although I had told my parents of my planned visit to these friends, I hadn't told them that I didn't know how I would travel to Thailand, nor where I would spend the night, as I hadn't wanted to worry them unnecessarily. But now I was suddenly unsure that it would all work out fine.

Various friends from my church were waiting at the airport to see me off and, after checking in, I had a bit of time to chat with them. When my flight was called and it was time to say good-bye, they all stood around me. We sang a song together and they sent me off with a prayer.

I didn't have any problems when I got through airport controls as I had feared I might have. After all, the prayers of my friends were accompanying me. I had just taken my seat when a family with two children came on board. The man was clearly Indian but the lady was white. They had the three seats next to me and another one on the other side of the gangway. The Indian man spoke to me in English and said, "Would you mind at all if you swapped seats with our boy?" I readily let him have my place so that the family could sit together during the long flight.

The passenger next to me was a young Arab lady, just 21, who had already been married for several years. She raved about her husband and how much she was looking forward to seeing him again. She got off the plane in Dubai leaving the window seat next to me empty.

Soon after take-off, the boy from the Indian family came across to me. He was about 9 or 10, and asked if he could sit next to the window. I was busy writing a few greeting cards but we had a little chat in English. He asked about this and that and suddenly I realised that we were speaking in German.

"How do you know German?" I asked him. He told me they had just been to visit their granddad in Germany and that they were now on their way back home to Kuala Lumpur. I pricked up my ears. He told me that his family lived in Kuala Lumpur and that he went to school there.

"Perhaps your daddy can help me find a hotel," I said.

"I am sure he could. But you could stay with us," he said amiably.

About two hours before we reached our destination I got chatting to his mum in the gangway. She and her husband were also involved in Christian work. I asked her about accommodation possibilities in Kuala Lumpur.

"I am sure my husband can help you there", she said.

When I approached him about it, he gave me the address of a YMCA[20] hostel. I was thankful that everything was working out so well.

Later on, when we get off the plane, we bumped into each other again.

"If you would like to, you could stay overnight with us," the lady suggested. "I have no idea what things will look like in our house, but we'd manage somehow." I gladly accepted her kind invitation and so got to experience an Asian welcome at their home. Even though it was already dark, half their family had appeared to welcome them. I didn't understand much of what was said as they spoke mainly in Hindi, but it felt so good to be there in the shelter of a family, and sheltered from taxi drivers you were never really sure you could trust. I didn't have to worry about anything. When I mentioned that I still needed a ticket for my connecting flight to Thailand the next day, the Indian man immediately sent his brother to get the ticket for me. The next day, they even gave me a lift to the airport.

God had answered our prayers in many wonderful ways.

---

[20] *YMCA* stands for *Young Men's Christian Association*, nowadays open to both men and women.

# Chapter 29

# Village Library

During the workshop I had attended in Irian Jaya during my first term, one of the things we had discussed was language acquisition. We were introduced to a five-tiered model in which the lowest tier stood for no knowledge at all of a given language, and the highest tier stands for the knowledge of a language at the level of a native speaker. It is extremely difficult for a foreigner to reach the highest tier.

The question we had to consider was which level someone had to reach in order to understand the Word of God. The answer would determine whether God's Word should be translated for a particular people group or whether they were able to understand the Bible sufficiently in the national language. Roughly speaking, level 2 is sufficient for daily life and market business. In order to understand the Gospels you'd need to be on level 3, and to be able to understand the New Testament Epistles you would probably need to understand the language at level 4.

My assessment of my own understanding of the Indonesian language at that point was that I was on tier 3 plus. In order to build up my language skills, I determined to keep working at it. I was not able to learn much more from the villagers as they themselves had not mastered the Indonesian language sufficiently well. So that my language skills didn't stagnate, I decided to read as much as possible, but there was next to no reading material to be found in that remote village. Every time I went to Java, I would go into various bookshops and buy Indonesian books on a variety of topics including interesting biographies. Some of those biographies described people whose lives had appeared to come to a dead end, but who had then met God and through faith had received a new hope and a new direction for their lives. A few months later I began to wonder if those biographies might help the young people in the village to expand their horizons a little and to gain a new perspective for their lives.

One day a young man came to visit and Renate introduced him to me. "This is Warin. He is visiting his family and wants to collect some medicine."

"What do you normally do?" I asked him.

"For the last few years I've been living in the mountains at Padang Ca-pau. I am tilling land there, because I want to plant coffee. There are a few other young people up there, but we are scattered about a bit."

"Isn't it boring up there? What do you do in the evenings?"

"Sometimes we visit one another. One of us has a radio, so we find out what is going on in the world. And if someone has something to read, then we all share it around."

I took note, as he immediately adds, "Would you have anything to read that I could borrow?"

And so a small library was born.

In the following weeks I kept a look out for books on topics that would interest the village youth. I discovered that more and more children's books, especially Bible comics, were coming on the market and were available in Christian bookshops. I extended my library offer to the children in the Sunday school and told them that they could come to me to borrow books, but none of them came. They were just not used to reading books.

"If you would like to read something nice, just come over," I invited the sons of Pak Kor, our pastor. "I have some interesting books with lovely pictures. Just come and have a look at them."

One afternoon in the holidays, I heard children's voices outside the front door. When I opened the door, five or six children were standing there.

"We want to look at the books," they said.

"Great! I'm pleased about that. Come on in." My heart was jubilant.

I spread mats on the floor and the children sat down. Then I took a pile of books and spread them out in front of them. "Here. Have a look at them. If you want to take one home to read, then tell me and I'll make a note of which one you borrow."

The children soon became engrossed in the books and were fascinated by the pictures. Each child chose a book to take home.

"I've made a note of the book each of you is taking home. Just be careful your younger brothers and sisters don't damage it. When you bring it back, then you can take another one home," I explained.

The ice was broken. Some of the children come back the next day bring-ing other children with them. This went on for several weeks. Needless to say, I made sure I expanded my stock of books.

I noticed one child in particular – Iwan, our neighbour's youngest son. He was only in year one at school. Whenever a group of children came to our house, he always tagged along with them. He would look at the pictures in the books with utter devotion, but he never took a book home. The long-ing in his eyes spoke volumes.

"You are allowed to borrow a book too," I told him.

"He can't read yet," the others said.

"That's OK." But still he never borrowed a book.

While I was in Germany for several months, Renate kept the library going. When I returned I brought more new books with me. Seven-year-old Iwan was the first one to borrow one of those books. He came every day, sometimes several times in a day. I was pleased that he had turned into a bookworm and was making good progress at school. Sadly, Iwan didn't grow up to become a diligent young man. He got into bad company and went off the rails. He became a burden to his mother, lazing around at home and without work.

But it made a difference in the lives of others. Jadi for example, who was an incredible bookworm, went to Bible school and became a pastor. Or Jonatan, one of the sons of our pastor, who became a pharmacist, told me how important that little library was for him as a child.

Chapter 30

# What about Our Story?

I heard the yard gate open. We had never oiled it and it saved getting a bell which no-one would use anyway. Through the window, I could see two men opening the gate. Our dogs, barking excitedly, rushed to the gate. Faced with the dogs, the men stopped abruptly. As Renate was in her room having her siesta, I opened the front door and greeted the men.

"We have come for treatment," they said.

"The clinic is closed at present but the nurse is at home. Please go over to the waiting area." I pointed to the covered porch in front of the clinic.

"Do we get a story as well?"

Obviously these two men knew that we liked to tell our waiting patients stories from the Bible and they wanted the full works. I assured them that I could tell them a story.

"Just wait a minute," they responded. "There are a few more people coming and they want to hear the story as well."

I looked down towards the village and could see a line of people coming up the path.

"Where are you from?" I asked the two men.

"From beyond Bengkulu. We left this morning, a whole car load of us, but it took longer than we thought."

Renate, who had been following the conversation from indoors, had got dressed and came out with the clinic key.

There were about 15 people and when everyone had sat down, I asked, "Do you really want to hear a story from the Bible?"

"Yes," they all chorused. They obviously considered medicine and stories went hand in hand for holistic treatment.

So I began with my story.

I told them how God's people had rebelled against God during their wanderings in the desert, complaining about their circumstances: no bread, no water, the heat and the never-ending manna. They were sick to the back teeth of that. God sent poisonous snakes among them and many of the people died. Others, however, came to their senses. They confessed their guilt and turned back to God. Now God didn't just eliminate the consequence of their rebellion, saying, "It's okay, it's no big deal." He wanted to help them and so He showed them the way to be saved. He got Moses to make a bronze snake and put it up on a stick so that everyone was able to see it. Now whoever was bitten, could look at the bronze snake, and not die. (You can read the full story in Numbers 21, verses 4-9).

"If we were bitten by a snake today, I guess we would not be convinced that we would be healed by looking at a bronze snake. I guess we would go to a clinic to get an injection. But at that point in time that was God's way of saving the people who had rebelled against Him and had complained about the conditions they found themselves in. Haven't we all done that at some point? Haven't we all rebelled against God and complained about our conditions in life? Which one of us can claim not to be guilty of rebelling against God? None of us, I expect. But God is not able to be in relationship with people who have turned away from Him, people who are sinful. The consequence of turning away from God is death; God's word tells us that. We all deserve death. And yet, God wants to enable people to have a meaningful relationship with Him. That is what He created us for. And so He gave us a way out: Jesus Christ took the consequences of our sin on Himself, so that every single person who believes in Him is not lost, but receives eternal life.

"Perhaps this solution seems as hard to understand as the solution with the bronze snake. But we are all guilty of turning away from God, and it is only when we look to Jesus that we are forgiven and our sin is no longer held against us. This is the way into a life of relationship with God."

The people had listened carefully. They seemed to have understood my story but they weren't yet ready to dare to make the step towards Jesus. Will I ever see any of them again? I don't know, but I am sure that an important seed had been sown.

Chapter 31

# A Visit to Patients in Padang Guci

It was the dry season and week after week patients came to the clinic from Padang Guci, the next big river valley south of Kedurang. There was always a taxi full, about 15 people. We were quite keen to have a look at how things were there, and when Renate was invited to visit by one of the patients, we gladly accepted the opportunity and Renate asked someone to explain to her how to get there.

This time, our pastor Pak Kor and his wife, our trainee student, my translation assistant Sida, and the teacher Pak Elias went with us. We set off after an early lunch. In Manna, the district town, we stopped, as usual, at the post office, the church, and the market. We bought rice and noodles, some vegetables and two chickens, as well as a big tin of biscuits as gifts.

The tarmacked coastal road was in good condition. South of Manna there was not a lot of traffic and at one point, as we went round a bend, we found a herd of cows sitting in front of us on the road. Renate braked sharply and came to a halt. She had to beep the horn before the herd eventually started to move. One after another, the animals heaved themselves up and ambled casually to the side of the road. We drove slowly past them.

After the turning to Kedurang, the road became narrower and the landscape wilder and less cultivated. It smelled of rainforest. We crossed small, rickety bridges over deep gorges. There was little water in the streams below the bridges. We drove past recently cleared forest areas where the land had been partly burnt. In the distance we saw a troop of monkeys. We rarely passed a village. Then suddenly, we were out of the jungle and saw the wide valley spread out in front of us with a river snaking through the middle. There wasn't much water in the river and so the valley was rather sandy. At several places we saw quarries where sand and gravel were being loaded onto lorries by hand to be sold as building materials.

This was the valley of Padang Guci. Slowly, we drove onto the long, wide bridge. Pak Kor was keen to tell us about the bridge. "This is the biggest bridge in the whole of the province and is about 600 metres long," he said. "The river turns into a fast flowing torrent during the rainy season, flooding the whole valley. The water flows with such force that it only mixes with the salt water of the sea about a kilometre into the ocean. You can see it from the plane. The bridge is still quite new but there were problems building it because the force of the water damaged it."

Awestruck, we drove over the big, strong, concrete bridge and on to higher ground. We saw a huge gum tree with its massive roots – though deeply anchored into the ground, the huge roots protruded out of the ground and appeared to prop up the branches. In the cool shade of this rainforest giant there were a few small stalls selling rice dishes, fried bananas, roasted peanuts and drinks. We took a break to stretch our legs, take some pictures and buy some fried bananas and roasted peanuts for the journey.

"Where do we have to turn off? Is it far to the turning?" we asked.

"You'll see. It's about five kilometres on."

Re-energised, we drove on. The turning was really not hard to miss, even though there were no signs anywhere. The road was in good condition. We drove upriver along the brow of the hill, but from there we couldn't see the river. After about 15 kilometres we took the turning to the village down by the river. What an incredible view of the river valley greeted us. We drove slowly down the track which would probably be quite tricky to drive on in the rainy season. It was late afternoon when we reached the village, thankful that we had arrived safely.

The village people showed us the way to the house of the family we were visiting. It was a small house, made of wood and bamboo and was built on narrow stilts almost two metres tall. We climbed the bamboo ladder which led up to the front door. Our hosts greeted us warmly. We unloaded our things and gave the groceries we had brought to the lady of the house, who accepted them gratefully and started cooking straight away.

The front room of the house was a long narrow room which extended across the whole width of the house. There was no furniture. Mats were spread out and we sat down. Next door in the kitchen the hostess was busy. Through the passage way we could see the open fireplace used for cooking. The walls were lined with various utensils and with sacks full of food stores. The kitchen was about as big as the front room, but was made of bamboo instead of wood, as bamboo is less flammable.

We were served a glass of cool water, which refreshed us, and we exchanged news.

As we wanted to freshen up a bit after our journey, we asked if there was a well where we could wash. "No," they replied. "We all go to the river to wash. The children can go with you to show you the bathing area."

Armed with a *basahan*[21], soap and a towel, as well as fresh clothing, we ladies walked in single file for about 300 metres across the wide, flat riverbank to the edge of the water. On the way to the river, more and more children joined us. They had never seen white women before. It was not long before we were surrounded by a gaggle of children. On the opposite riverbank there were rocks and some children were climbing up them and then, with great excitement, jumping into the water. They were swept quite a distance downstream before they managed to clamber back on land. Although the river was not very wide at that place, the current was strong.

I was not used to bathing with a *basahan* and was afraid of losing my cloth in the current, so I decided to wash wearing my loose dress. That worked fine, until I wanted to dry myself and get changed. As I struggled to get it off over my head, the wet cotton of the dress clung to my skin. The children stared at me and were probably wondering why I was so clumsy. I realised that using the *basahan* would be a lot more comfortable, as you could tie your towel over the top and pull the *basahan* away underneath.

Back at the house, we decided to visit the village head to register according to regulations. Pak Kor went with us. We walked through the whole village to get to the man's house. It was a large, traditional wooden house with a big veranda. We climbed up and sat down. When the village head arrived, we recognised him immediately. He was the taxi driver who regularly brought patients to our clinic. Immediately, there was a mutual degree of trust, and we were soon chatting together. We were really happy we had been able to make this visit, but didn't want to stay too long as we needed to get back to our host family before darkness fell.

A few of our former patients were waiting to greet us at our hosts' home. We sat together on mats on the floor and the small room soon filled up. Most people didn't stay long as they also wanted to get home for their evening meal, but promised to come back later in the evening. When everyone had gone, we, too, were able to eat and took time to enjoy our meal. The hostess had made a tasty dish with the chickens. Afterwards, as we sat comfortably in a circle, we were served sweet tea. Suddenly, there was a disturbance in the kitchen next door.

"Did you bring sugar?" the host asked.

Renate and I looked at each other and, somewhat unsure of ourselves, shook our heads. "No, we didn't."

---

[21]  A *basahan* is a cloth or piece of material which you wrap around yourself and tuck together over the breast when you wash in public. You can soap off underneath.

"Are you absolutely sure you didn't bring sugar?"

"Yes, we're sure. Why?"

The hostess was standing in the doorway with a half empty bag of sugar which she held out to us.

"Are you sure you didn't bring this sugar? Someone brought it round earlier and said it was in the back of your car."

"No, we really didn't bring sugar. And anyway, we had completely unloaded the car."

Our hosts appeared even more unsettled than before. Quickly, they collected our half empty glasses and poured the tea away.

"Why are they pouring away the tea?" I asked, puzzled.

"They are afraid that someone wants to poison us," the pastor explained. "That does happen in this area."

Not long afterwards the first visitors arrived. As more and more came, we left the pastor to chat to the men and joined the women in the kitchen. A few women asked Renate for medicine for themselves or their children. She had only brought a limited selection, and said, "You'll have to come to me at the clinic."

"I've been to your clinic once," one of the women told me.

"Were we able to help you?" I asked.

"Yes, I soon got better."

"That's good. Did you get to hear a story as well?"

"Yes," she replied, and then told me the Bible story she had heard during her visit at the clinic. I hadn't expected her to remember it so clearly.

"I also brought a booklet with stories home with me," she added. "I take it with me to my rice field every day and read it during my break."

We continued to chat a bit longer and I tried to answer some of her questions.

It was late when the last visitors left. It was arranged that the men would sleep in the front room and the ladies in the kitchen. We lay on mats next to each another and covered ourselves with our thin batik cloths. There were even a few pillows. It was surprisingly cold in the river valley especially as the moist night air crept in through the wide slits in the bamboo wall. Pak Kor's wife was lying next to me. Her feet were freezing cold and she tried to warm them up on me. I let her. I didn't expect to sleep much anyway. On the way home the next day, as we drove through the beautiful countryside, she thanked me for my "hot water bottle" service. We reminisced about the visit and shared our impressions of all that had taken place. Pak Kor admitted he had felt sick when he heard that the sugar in our tea had come from an unknown source. I certainly didn't seem to have suffered any adverse effects, even though I had almost drained my glass.

# Chapter 32

# The Kidnapped Bride

"Merin kidnapped a bride during the night!"
Our neighbours called out the news to us as they walked past our house to the public well.

It was still early in the morning, only about half past six. We had just finished breakfast and were busy washing up behind the house. Nenek Wil and Nenek Wini, the two grandmothers who had stayed the night with us, were not too concerned by this news.

"What happened?"

"Merin has kidnapped a bride for himself."

I was still not sure that I had understood correctly as no-one seemed to be unduly worried about this news. They explained to me what happened.

"He brought the girl home with him. She will have come willingly. There will be a wedding soon." It was clear that this was a happy turn of events.

"And that is okay?" I asked, somewhat surprised.

"Well, of course," Nenek Wini laughs. "He brought the girl home to his mother. That's what we do here. I was kidnapped too."

I looked at her incredulously.

"Honestly! The wedding will probably be arranged in a matter of weeks. The dowry is not that high."

"What happens now?" I asked, curious.

"Well," they explained, "normally, they will have both agreed to this. The girl will have left a note behind, with a clue as to her whereabouts. Then the girl's family has to make contact with the young man's family. Once they have come to an agreement, they have the wedding. The young man doesn't touch the girl before the wedding, but places her into the care of his mother."

We chatted a bit longer about this custom. On their way home, the two ladies stopped to visit our neighbours, Merin's parents, to greet the young bride.

Later, I found out that the girl came from a village about 15 kilometres upriver. The two young people had met at a celebration the evening before. Merin's friend had also met a girl. After the party, the four of them had walked back through the dark night. I found it hard to understand that these two young girls had no problem about following strange men with a view of marrying them. Merin had even told her that he was a Christian and that he wanted to marry the Christian way. The girl didn't have a problem with that either. "The main thing is I get married," she had replied. Incredible!

A few days later, I ask what the outcome of it all was.

"Well, the girl's family came. They wanted a water buffalo as dowry", but Merin responded, "That's not possible. It is much too expensive but if you insist on it, then the girl will have to return home." But the girl didn't want to go home."

The families must have reached some sort of agreement because a few weeks later their wedding took place.

# Chapter 33

# Built on Rock

I was sitting on the mat in the living room and, as on most evenings, was reading to the older ladies out of my translated Bible texts. That day the text was about the wise and foolish builders portrayed at the end of the Sermon on the Mount in Matthew 7.

"The wise man builds his house on *batu*." *Batu* is the Serawai word for rock or stone.

At that point Nenek Wil interrupted me. "How can you build a house on a *batu*? It's not possible," she insisted. She had obviously been listening intently, and yet the story wasn't making any sense to her.

I was surprised and thought for a minute. In most translations it says that the wise man built his house on a rock, implying a big block of rock. In this whole area, however, there were no big rock faces. As the Serawai language has neither a definite nor indefinite article, "to build on stone" could equally mean "to build on a stone". So she was completely right. You can't build a house on a stone, especially if you are thinking of a normal stone that you can pick up with your hands.

"Well," I quickly started to explain, "It was not just a normal little stone. It was a great big stone, so big you could fit a house on it." I used my arms to demonstrate what I meant.

But they just shook their heads. "Who is going to climb up something like that?" they demanded incredulously.

"Help!" I thought. "How am I meant to explain to these people, who have never seen a rock, what a rock is?" Out loud I said, "Well, it wasn't just a big stone, but it was like – you know – like a mountain of stone."

The ladies just fell about laughing. "No-one would pile up so many stones as to make a mountain of stone. And anyway, how would you build a house on top of that. That's nonsense. Nobody would ever do that!"

They were, of course, right. In the way they understood it, it just did not make sense. In Indonesian you can give weight to a plural by repeating the word again, but in Serawai, if it is clear from the context that a word is already in the plural, repeating the word adds no more weight to it. As there was no single stone as big as a mountain in this whole area, to them it had to be an accumulation of stones. I had obviously failed to explain to them what a rock was. I was at a loss to know how I could explain it so, for the rest of the evening, we turned to something else.

The next day I talked the problem over with my translation helper, Sida. She also had no further advice to give. In the evening, when the ladies came back, I tried again. The traditional houses in this area of Sumatra are built of wood on top of thick wooden pillars.

"Where would you build a house so that it was safe from floods?" I asked the ladies.

"On a *cugung*," was their prompt answer. A *cugung* is a longish hill, a little like a dune.

"But then you get the wind blowing at it," someone objected.

For every suggestion they made, someone else raised an objection. We were obviously not getting any nearer to a solution.

The next day I decided to look at the whole of the text again. This story is a parable. At the end of the Sermon on the Mount, Jesus compares those who listen to what he is saying and the way they respond to it, to a wise and a foolish builder. The houses refer to the human life that should be based on strong foundations, in other words the Word of God, so that when difficulties and crises come, it doesn't cave in or fall apart. Perhaps, that was where the key lay.

In the evening, the grandmothers were there again. The women were not the ones who built houses – that was men's business after all – but perhaps they knew something about house building anyway. So I asked them, "What do you do so that your houses don't wobble, but are stable and strong?"

"Well, you know," they answered, "we put a stone underneath the pillars."

It was my turn to look at them in surprise and disbelief. "Sometimes we even put three stones under the pillar," someone else added quickly. "We also do that so that the pillars don't stand in the wet and begin to rot."

"So why didn't you understand when I read that a house needed to be built on stone?"

"Oh, we don't call that stone a *batu*."

"What do you call it then?"

"It's called *pelapiak*[22]."

I noted down the word immediately so that I wouldn't forget it.

When Sida came to work the next day, we took this expression and worked it into the text. "The wise man builds his house on a foundation of

---

[22] *Pelapiak* means foundation.

101

stone and the foolish man builds his house on a foundation of sand," we framed the sentence.

In the evening, I read the new version of the story to the ladies. They nodded in agreement and all conceded, "Exactly. That is what the wise man does."

1. The small Batak church in Bengkulu (Introduction)

2. Our house in the village of Napal Melintang (Chapter 9)

3. Looking down from the house towards the village and church (Chapter 9)

4. The village street through Napal Melitang (Chapter 9)

5. I learn how to weave baskets (Chapter 9)

6. A feast (Chapter 10)

7. Plate dance
(Chapter 10)

8. Between the grandmothers (Chapter 11)

9. Praperation (Chapter 17)

10. The children carrying the grocery to the house (Chapter 20)

11. With Renate on the motorbike (Chapter 20)

12. Spectators in front of the window (Chapter 24)

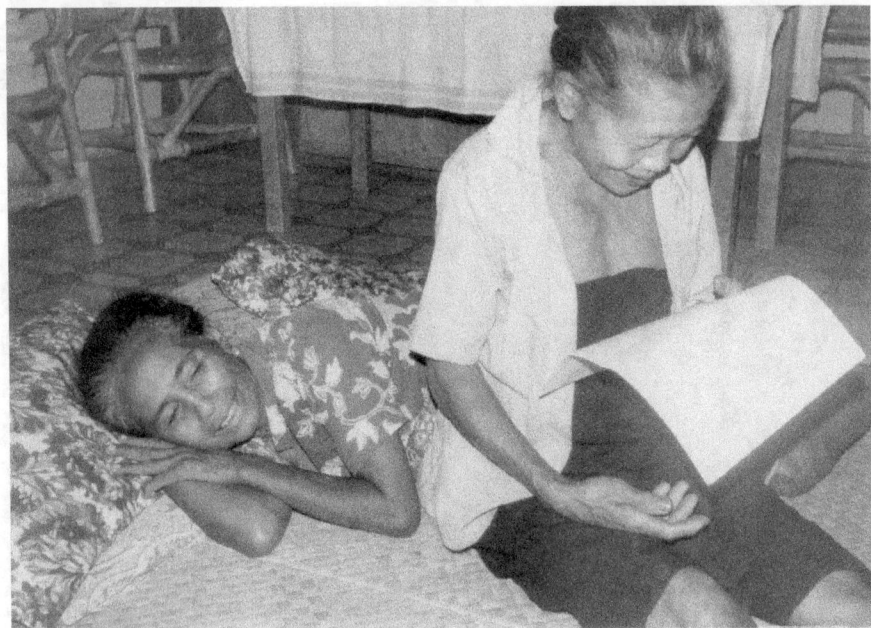

13. Nenek Wini reading the translated text to the others (Chapter 26)

14. Children borrowing books (Chapter 29)

15. Typical village house (Chapter 34)

16. „Peter the Great" getting his bottle (Chapter 35)

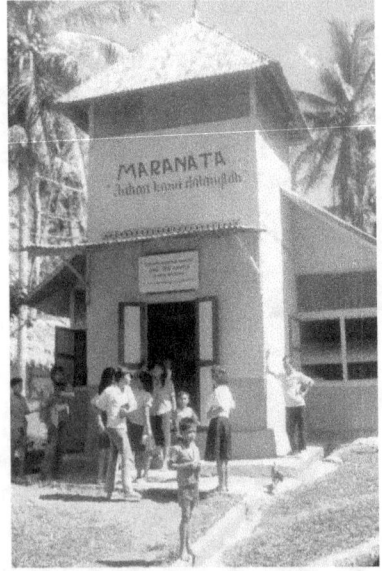

17. The village church (Chapter 9)

18. Checking the translated text with the Serawai people (Chapter 37)

19. Translating together with Sida (Chapter 44)

20. Checking the text with the consultant from the Bible Society

21. Grandmothers sleeping in the living room

22. Fellowship at the beach (Chapter 48)

23. Sida in Kalimantan at the Kapuas River (Chapter 54)

24. Loading the car for the move (Chapter 58)

25. Pak Mahar singing at the Christmas celebration (Epilogue)

26. Official handover of the Serawai NT by the Indonesian Bible Society, March 1995

Chapter 34

# Dream or Nightmare

In the meantime, a few of the young families from our village had moved to Padang Capau up in the mountains to start a new life there. They invited us to visit them some day and to have a service together. Although they had told us that there was not yet a road up to the area, we decided we should go. One day, Renate and I set off, accompanied by some others. About 30 km before Bengkulu, we had to turn off from the coastal road onto the Suka Raja rubber plantation. A mosque and a small wooden church had been built in front of the plantation management office, next to the administration building, but the site was still bare as no rubber trees had yet been planted. We had visited the Christians there several times in the past and had worshipped with them. On this occasion, too, we stopped and went into one of the houses for a short visit with the family.

When we drove on, we passed recently cultivated sites. The trees were still small. The drive continued through fairly hilly countryside before we reached some wooden barracks. The Riman family from our village had been living there for a while. We left the car at their house and someone took us to the tiny market at Talang Tebat at the foot of the Barisan mountain range. We travelled through a thick forest of rubber trees where the trees were lined up tightly, like tin soldiers. This was the older part of the plantation. The trunks had been slashed, and bamboo receptacles had been placed at the bottom of each tree to catch the sap as it dripped out.

From Talang Tebat, we still had to walk a good ten kilometres to reach our destination. The wide mud road was steep, but the higher we climbed, the more beautiful the view. Below us lay the huge plantation and we could recognise the different barracks in which the workers lived. In the distance we could see the coast. The path was wide and took us over the tops of the mountains. In between the summits the path descended steeply, only to ascend just as steeply on the other side. The sun was burning brightly and we began to sweat. We were pleased that at various huts along the path we were able to get drinking water and refresh ourselves. The wide path ended about two kilometres from our destination and a small track led onwards through the rainforest. The tall trees provided shade, and it became noticeably cooler. By then it was late afternoon and the mosquitoes had woken up and were causing mischief!

At last we arrived at a clearing with several huts and were excitedly welcomed by some of our acquaintances. We asked where the others were.

"They are bathing," they said.

"Down by the river?" I asked. I knew that would be quite a way to walk as the river was far below us. I was worried that we might have to go down the steep hill to wash.

"No," they replied. "We have a spring here with lots of clear water. We have even installed a bamboo pipe. You can stand under the water that comes out and have a proper shower. You will like it. Why don't you go now? The women are there at the moment. The men will bathe later."

When Renate and I, armed with our *basahan*, soap and a towel, arrived at the water place we met some of the women. How surprised they were to see us!

"You really came!" they greeted us in amazement. "We didn't dare believe that you would. But now you are here." Everyone was speaking at once.

"How do you like our shower?"

"It is really amazing. We don't even have anything like this in the village."

"Why don't you try it out? Stand underneath," they urged us and stepped aside.

After our tiring walk, the cold mountain water felt wonderful on my hot body. It was so refreshing and I felt newly born.

We were invited to change in one of the huts which had two little rooms; the smaller one was the kitchen and had a fire place and various sacks of food stores. There was not a single piece of furniture in the whole house.

When it got dark, we were served a delicious meal. Afterwards people from the other houses came to visit. They wanted to hear all the latest news from the village. Then we had a service together.

That night we slept close together in the kitchen with the ladies of the house. An extra layer of bamboo had been laid out over the floor in the sleeping area and acted as some sort of insulation but it was still cold as the walls of the bamboo huts provided little protection. As usual, I had only my *kain*[23] with me as a cover and could hardly sleep because of the cold and the hard floor. The next morning, the sun quickly warmed up my tired limbs.

---

[23] A *kain* is a batik cloth, a good two metres long, which Javanese women wrap around themselves as a skirt.

Soon after breakfast, we said goodbye. Our visit had been something really special for our friends up there in the mountains.

"Come again soon!" they called out as we left them.

It was a few months later...

"I want to visit our friends in the mountains again." Renate was already working out her travel plans. "This time I am going to go by car," she said. "The path was wide enough for a car and it was in good condition. I am told, too, that it has been extended nearly up to the houses in Padang Capau."

"And if it rains?" I queried. "Then we'll be stuck. Not even our four-wheel drive would manage those steep slopes."

But for Renate everything had been decided. It was the dry season and the weather was fine. First we drove to Bengkulu to visit the Dandra family. Pak Dandra was the district pastor and we often stayed overnight at their home. Renate invited Ibu Dandra, the pastor's wife, to join us and our three other passengers.

The road to Talang Tebat had been reinforced with gravel and the mud path leading up into the mountains was still in good condition. It was so much more comfortable making the journey sitting in a car. I had made sure, too, that I had a warmer cloth with me to use as a blanket in the night. During the few months since we last came, more forest had been cleared. There were also more huts along the path. When the path came to an end, we got out. There was a turning point there and we were able to park the car by the side of the road. The final 500 metres on foot were a piece of cake.

When we reached the clearing, I noticed straight away that there were now more huts. There also seemed to be more children. After we had had a refreshing shower, our host said, "We are all invited for dinner at Pak Inri's house. He lives ten minutes up the hill. Let's go before it is dark." It was a tricky climb up the tiny footpath between the young coffee bushes which were growing on the slopes. I was glad I had taken my torch with me for the walk down.

The Inri family greeted us warmly. There were other guests too. They wanted us to have a service together and asked me to give the message. Well, good that they told me ahead of time! We sat together in a circle on mats on the floor and someone handed me a Bible.

The meal was served after the service. As usual for a small party, a few chickens had been killed and cooked in coconut milk. We also had rice and vegetable dishes prepared with unripe papayas and sweet potato leaves. It was delicious. But then my mood dropped. I could hear that it had started to rain.

"How are we going to get away tomorrow?" I whispered to Renate.

She was not that worried. "Once the sun comes out tomorrow morning," she reassured me, "the path will dry up quickly as it is not in the shade."

"Why don't you stay here for the night," our hosts suggested. "It won't be much fun going down through the wet coffee grove in the dark. We wouldn't want you to slip and break any bones."

They were right. No matter that all our overnight things were in the valley, the steep climb down on the wet mud would have been treacherous for us city people. We readily agreed and stayed on the mountain for the night. They gave us women a small hut next door which had a spacious bamboo floor. A few mats were spread out and we were even given a couple of small pillows. I thought regretfully of my warm cloth down in the valley. The moist air had already turned cold.

"Is there anything else you need?" our hostess asked. "There are still a few more mats."

"Oh, yes please," I replied.

I took another mat and used it as a covering. Even though it was a stiff grass mat, it kept off the cold, moist air and warmed me surprisingly well. Nevertheless, I didn't sleep a lot. I kept waking up, hearing the soft pitter-patter of the rain drops. I would have preferred a torrential downpour as that drains away quickly, but with the light rain the water would seep into the ground and soften the soil. I wondered how many days we would have to stay before the path was dry enough to drive on.

Morning came at last. Heavy clouds were still hanging low in the sky but the rain had stopped. After a coffee we dared to make the descent through the coffee grove. The bushes were dripping wet and the soil was soft and very slippery. I noticed that the local people simply squatted down and slid down the steep, slippery bits on their feet. I decide to copy them, but immediately landed on my bottom. Thankfully, I reached the huts pretty much in one piece.

"How long do you think we are going to have to wait before we can dare to drive home?" I asked Renate.

"I think we should just try it. It is drying off fairly well. We'll manage," she replied with conviction.

I had my doubts but followed her instructions. The ladies had boiled some rice and soon after breakfast we set off for home. Two of the people who had come with us were staying, but three others wanted to hitch a lift back to the village. They had a few sacks of luggage with them which we loaded into the back of the car. Renate switched on the four wheel drive and, after a prayer for God's help and protection, we set out.

That far up in the mountains there were no shady spots. Even though the sun was still behind the clouds, the path had dried off fairly well. Nevertheless, Renate drove carefully and we made surprisingly good headway. Then we approached a steep descent with an even steeper ascent on the other side. The overloaded car began to stall as we started our climb. On our left was a sheer drop into the valley below. Horrified, I realised that if we stalled there, we would most certainly slide backwards down the slope. Renate put her foot down on the accelerator, but the wheels only spun on the mud. We could feel the tension rise in the car.

"Dalam nama Yesus! In the name of Jesus!"

One of the men spoke these words out loud. As if by an invisible hand, the car seemed as though it was pushed along until the wheels gripped the road again and we managed to drive up the ascent.

"Thank you, Jesus!" We all breathed a sigh of relief and sang a song of praise.

Renate drove on slowly. It seemed that we had got over the worst. We were back on the ridge, and from there the ups and downs would be gentler. Finally, we reached the steep descent to Talang Tebat, some 100 metres away. On the right hand side of the road there was a sheer drop. There were a few trees by the side of the road and in their shade the red mud was as slippery as black ice. Renate decided to change to first gear. She slowed down, almost to a halt and the engine cut out. The car began to slide towards the drop on the right. The men got out. One of them tried to support the car from the right, but could not get a good enough foothold for himself.

"I'm not able to start the engine," Renate said. "If I go into neutral we will slip." The handbrake in that car had never worked.

"I'll see what I can do," I promised as I got out of the car.

The ground was so slippery that I had to hold on to the car to stop myself from sliding.

"I can hardly stay upright," I called, "and I can't see any stones or wood lying around. What shall I do?" I didn't have the slightest idea.

Renate had an idea. "We have ropes in the car, don't we? Could you tie the car to a tree so that I can at least start the engine?"

I got the ropes, doubled them up and tried to attach one end to a tree growing at the side of the mountain. The slope was so steep that it was impossible for me to climb up to reach it. A thin tree, no thicker than my forearm, was the only one I could reach. I fastened one end of the rope to it, pulled it tight and fastened the other end to the car.

"Right, now you can try," I signalled to Renate.

She put the gear into neutral; the car slipped and I watched in horror as the little tree bent right over and fell into the road.

"Stop! The rope is not holding!" I shrieked.

"I did it! Hallelujah!" I heard Renate shout. "You can get back in now." But none of the men wanted to get back in.

As I unfastened the ropes, I said, "I'll come with you, Renate. If we slide down into the ravine, at least we'll be together." To be honest, I knew I would feel safer in the car than trying to slide my way down the mountain. As soon as I was sitting next to her in the car, I asked, "How did you manage to start the engine? The ropes were not holding."

"They did for a short moment. That was enough to start up the engine."

When we had arrived safely back in the village, Renate commented drily, "It was a dream of mine to go up into the mountains to Padang Capau with the car before I leave Sumatra." Renate was due to leave the country a few weeks later.

"For me it was more of a nightmare," was my reply.

# Chapter 35

# Peter the Great

Sida had gone into the forest with the Sunday school children who wanted to collect greenery for the Christmas tree. The next day, she showed me something which looked like a ball of checkered wool.

She held the ball out to me and I was startled when I saw two eyes blinking at me.

"What is it?"

"It's a *setuau rebang*[24]."

*Setuau* is the Serawai word for tiger. I knew that already but I was not familiar with a *setuau rebang* . So I asked her how big it would get.

"Not much bigger than a cat," she assured me.

"Where did you get it?"

"The children found it in the forest yesterday."

I looked at the animal more closely. It looked like a kitten but had round ears and its fur was checkered, like a leopard's. The animal was trembling with fear and hissed at us. It was probably no more than two weeks old and could hardly stand on its wobbly legs. Apart from that it seemed to be fine. I wondered why the mother abandoned it for it still needed her milk.

"How did you find it?"

"The nest was hidden in the tall grass. We almost stepped on it. There were three of these little creatures and the children took them all."

"How ever are they supposed to survive? They need their mother."

"That's why I am bringing it to you. One of them is already dead."

"What was it fed with?"

"Bananas."

I had already discovered that bananas were seen as milk substitute in Sumatra. Even newborn babies were given bananas if there was no milk. And now, Sida and the children wanted me to provide this little leopard kitten with milk. Well, I could but try. Anything else would mean its certain death.

The easiest way would be to find a "foster mum". A few days earlier, we had given away our young kittens, and our cat still had a bit of milk. As cats

---

[24] *Setuau rebang* is the Serawai word for leopard cat.

will sometimes adopt other kittens as their own, I wondered if she might look after this strange kitten and suckle it. It was worth a try if nothing else. When Miezi came home, I introduced our new house mate to her straight away and held the ball of fluff under her nose. She sniffed at it. As if struck by lightning, she darted away. The first try had failed miserably.

It was obvious that I would have to feed it myself. Renate brought me a tin of baby milk from the clinic and I prepared some – but how was I going to feed it to the kitten? Renate suggested using a syringe and fetched one from the clinic. I drew up some milk and let the kitten suck the end of the syringe – a poor imitation of a cat's nipples. It didn't seem to work well, but with a little pressure from my thumb some milk did come out and the kitten managed to drink. However, if too much milk came out it choked and the milk ran down its chin or into its nose, making it sneeze. But the main thing was, it was getting some milk. In the evening, when my cats came home for dinner, I tried again to push the kitten on to my cat. While Miezi was eating, I held the kitten to her nipples. Miezi refused to cooperate and hissed at us.

But I didn't give up. The next day I tried again. I calmed my cat, stroked her and tried to distract her. On the third day, she finally allowed the little one to suck but she had already run out of milk. In other words, I was the one who was stuck with being the foster mum. That evening, when the grandmothers visited us, I showed them the newest member of our family.

"O my goodness, a *setuau*!" They looked quite frightened.

"But it isn't a *setuau*," I told them. "It's only a *setuau rebang*."

"It is still a *setuau*," they insisted.

There used to be tigers in the forests in that area and the people still lived in awe of them. In the Serawai culture, there is an occult meaning attached to the tiger. There are people with particular occult abilities who have their own personal tiger to protect them. If they come across it, they know it is their tiger. It can be dangerous to others, but not to them. Ceremonially, they have to feed it regularly with a boiled egg. That was how it was explained to me anyway.

"What do you want with this *setuau*? It is only going to chase your chickens."

I realised they were not interested in making friends with this animal so I took it outside in its box.

But it seemed the kitten had come to stay with us, and it needed a name. After all that the ladies had said that evening, I thought "Ivan the Terrible" might be appropriate. But there was no way I could really use that name as our neighbour's son was called Iwan. So I called him "Peter the Great" and sometimes talked affectionately about "my little Peter".

Caring for Peter the Great wasn't easy. Every few hours I had to give him the "bottle". Sometimes he had diarrhoea. After all, baby milk was not designed for him and I had apparently got the proportions wrong. His stomach should have been massaged and his fur, which was getting more and more tangled, should have been brushed by his mother's rough tongue. I just couldn't give him the kind of care his mother would have given, but the little fellow was growing. I tried to teach him to lap his milk but he would only step onto the dish it was in and play around in it. I pressed his little nose into the milk, but he just didn't seem to understand that he could be licking up the milk.

It only took a few days before he accepted me totally as his mother. He slept outside, hiding somewhere under a pile of wood, but as soon as I walked in the front door he would come running to the back door wanting to come to me. Sometimes I let him into my room and played with him as I would with a kitten, but his teeth and claws were very sharp and my hands quickly got all scratched up. He seemed to have an extremely good sense of smell and anything that had my smell on it had a magic appeal for him. For example, he would get my used tissues out of the bin and play with them. He was able to busy himself with a ball of scrunched up, sweaty smelling paper until the floor was covered in tiny shreds of paper.

One evening, I showed the ladies how little Peter played with the paper ball and would run after a piece of thread.

"It plays just like a cat," they said with surprise.

They were amused by his antics, how he would run about, jump in the air and get himself all in a twist.

Then suddenly, they came to their senses. "No, it's not a cat, it's a setuau," they said and refused to have anything more to do with him.

Feeding Peter the Great was a big challenge especially as he never learnt to lap milk for himself. The time came when he started to need solids. His mother would certainly have brought him small animals to eat. However, we hardly had any meat in the village and our cats and dogs were fed on rice mixed with a little bit of dried, salted fish. But Peter was having none of that. Eventually, I discovered that he would eat scrambled egg with rice and that became his staple diet. By the time Peter the Great was about two months old, he had become a lively, inquisitive little animal.

Then one weekend Renate and I had to go away for three days. On our return, as we walked up the path to our house, Enam, the 10 year old son of our neighbour, Pak Ria, came running up to me.

"Peter is dead," he said.

"Dead? What happened?"

111

"Last night he got into our hen house. The hens were so restless that we went down and hit out at whatever was there. In the dark we didn't see that it was your Peter."

"Did you eat him?"

"No!" He looked at me, horrified.

"It's all right," I assured him, "and thanks for letting me know."

I very much regretted that Peter the Great hadn't survived his first and only attempted hunting tour.

# Chapter 36

# A Loose Connection

I had become the proud owner of a small laptop computer. I had never dreamed that only ten years after gaining my IT degree I would be sitting in Sumatra, in a village with no electricity, yet with my very own computer. It had a small screen revealing eight lines, a built-in printer for printing on thermal paper, and an external disc drive. Using a special cable it was even possible to store data on a tape in a tape recorder.

The majority of Bible translators who took part at the workshop in Irian Jaya, used this model. The programmes that had been specially developed for Bible translation worked perfectly on it, which was why I had chosen it. I had also been told that I could contact the SIL technician at any time if I had any problems.

We had our own diesel engine generator to supply electricity to our house in the village. It also supplied electricity to the church, the pastor's house and another ten houses. Every evening, shortly after six o'clock, a man from the village came to start up the generator and we turned it off again at ten. Once in a while it would fail to work and the village people would sort it out. I often found this arrangement was too erratic and frustrating, so, to ensure the electricity supply for my computer, I decided to buy a solar cell in Jakarta. I attached it to the roof of our house and the electricity generated by the sun was stored in a car battery from which I was able to run my laptop. That meant I was not affected by any problems relating to the generator.

The computer made my work so much easier. When I corrected translated texts, I no longer had to type out the whole of the text again, but simply enter the changes. However, it was the thermal paper that proved problematic as it would turn black if left in the sun, and over time the writing would fade. On top of that, the sweat from my fingers would leave quite obvious fingerprints on the paper.

My joy over the computer, however, was short-lived: there seemed to be problems with the disc drive which worked at times and didn't at others. It was very annoying. I thought that there was probably a loose connection, but I couldn't work out where it was or whether there might be some other cause for the problem.

One day, I had a surprise visit from two German students, one of whom was studying civil engineering and the other electrical engineering. I told them about my problem with the disc drive. The electrical engineer was very interested and asked if I had a layout of the electronics. I got out the documents which not only contained a detailed layout of the electronics, but also drawings relating to the building of the machine.

"Do you think you can use this and perhaps find the fault?"

"I can't promise, but I can try," he said confidently, as he set about taking my disc drive apart down to the smallest components.

After a while I asked if he had found anything.

"No, nothing yet," he said, disappointed.

Then he began the laborious work of putting it all together again. When, after two hours, he had finally finished, there were two screws left over and the disc drive wasn't working any better than before.

I decided to write to the SIL technician in Irian Jaya to ask if he was familiar with the problem and whether he could perhaps give me some advice. Three weeks later I received a reply suggesting that if I had not done so yet, I should clean the write-head of the machine. That seemed like a good idea but I wondered how I should do it. I couldn't imagine getting very far with a cotton bud and methylated spirits which was what I used regularly to clean my tape recorder. I sent another letter. Three weeks later I receive the answer which advised me that cleaning discs were readily available in any computer shop.

"Great," I thought, "only there are no computer shops here in the jungles of Sumatra and the nearest one is in Jakarta, a 24-hour bus journey away." I wondered whether I knew anyone in Jakarta who could help me, but soon dismissed the idea. Instead, I wrote to my father in Germany, who had only to cross the road to go to his nearest computer shop, and asked him to get a cleaning disc for me. I knew I should receive it in a little over three weeks.

As it was just before Christmas and we were busy with Christmas celebrations, I shelved the translation work for a little while. It was already the beginning of February when I finally held the long-awaited cleaning disc from Germany in my hands. I did the cleaning process twice, just to be sure, but, unfortunately, nothing changed – the problem was still there.

Meanwhile three months had past. Finally, I decided to send the disk drive to the SIL technician in Irian Jaya. So, I carefully packed it and sent it to him, asking him to repair it. I received another drive by return of post so that I could continue to work unhindered.

Why hadn't I done that right away? Hindsight is a wonderful thing!

Chapter 37

# No Pain, no Gain

I had had the first small leaflets with Bible texts in the Serawai language printed. These leaflets included several parables and miracles and an outline, put together from the different Gospels, of the life and death of Jesus. As the first complete book of the Bible to translate, I chose the Gospel of John because it uses only a limited vocabulary, contains a lot of dialogue and brings people face-to-face with the deity of Jesus in a unique way.

When I made a start on it with my translation helper Sida, I realised that there were more problems with its translation than I had anticipated. To begin with, we skipped the prologue in chapter one with its theological assertions and looked at the story following it. In it, a delegation from Jerusalem asked Jesus who he was. At once, as in many subsequent dialogues, the question came up: how did Jesus address the people and how did they address him? In Serawai, an older person addresses a younger person differently from the way in which a younger person addresses an older person. Assuming that Jesus was in his early thirties, it was not always evident whether the people he was speaking to were older or younger. For example, Nicodemus (chapter 3) belonged to the Jewish Council but that did not necessarily mean that he was older than Jesus. Was the woman at the well (chapter 4) in her twenties or already in her thirties? Was she older or younger than Jesus?

We faced another problem when we came to the word "bread" (chapter 6). In this context, Jesus said about himself, "I am the bread of life." The Serawai people might know the word *roti*, the Indonesian word for bread, but very few of them had ever seen bread, let alone tasted it. In our local villages, the word *roti* was also used to refer to the dry biscuits that were served at celebrations. But Jesus is not this extra serving at celebrations! No, Jesus is the basic staple food without which we cannot live. For the Serawai people, however, that would be rice. But Jesus did not say, "I am the rice of the world." We finally solved the problem by using the general word for food. We faced a similar problem when we reached the vine (chapter 15). This time there was no misunderstanding and we borrowed the Indonesian word *anggur*.

After about four months of hard work, we had finished the draft transla-tion of the Gospel. We revised the text several times and looked at difficult expressions again. We also carefully compared the text with the original text to make sure that no phrase or word had been missed out and that each statement remained true to the original. I often read it out loud to the older ladies who slept in our house with the aim of finding out, through my ques-tions, how they had received the text and whether they had understood what it was saying. Before the Gospel was printed, I wanted to check it thor-oughly with regard to clarity, intelligibility and the natural flow of the lan-guage.

During a visit in Bengkulu, I chatted about it with Pak Yakardin who came from Kedurang. He had graduated from Bible school in Batu and was leading the social outreach of the church.

"It's important to make sure that there are no expressions in the text which would appear offensive to people in other areas," he said.

"Can that happen?" I asked, surprised.

"Yes, it can. The differences in the language between Pino and Maras are not just in the 'au' and 'o' word endings. There are also individual words that are only used in some areas and are regarded as offensive in other re-gions."

"I had no idea that could happen. Then we really need to check it thor-oughly with representatives from each area."

"Yes, that would be the safest. Perhaps we could all meet up and work through the text together," he suggested.

"That's a good idea. It would take a few days though. Do you think peo-ple would sign up for it?"

"Why not? If you invite them and pay for their travel, they will come."

We agreed on a date and planned four days of work. In the church, where we were going to work, we set up desks in a horseshoe shape. All the in-vited representatives from Kedurang, Siginim, Maras and our village, ar-rived on time. Together with Sida and myself, there were eight people in all.

We began by eating lunch, which our *neneks* had cooked for us, at my house. Then we went down to the church to work. Everyone had a copy of the Bible text in front of them. Most of them were not used to reading in Serawai, their mother tongue, and at the beginning stumbled in their read-ing. We alternated reading the whole of the paragraph out loud to get a gen-eral impression of the text and a feel for the context with reading a section sentence by sentence, asking ourselves what was not clear, what didn't sound natural, or how it could be expressed in a better way. Often the men would say, "It sounds a bit funny" but were not able to explain why. Then I would try to suggest improvements by moving parts of the sentence around, the way I had been taught when I was learning grammar analysis.

"Yes, that sounds much better," they'd reply. "Ibu Hildegard knows our language so much better than we do."

"No, that's not true. I am only playing with the words. Only you can judge when the sentence really sounds right."

It was laborious, time-consuming work which demanded a lot of concentration for each of us. We made slow progress but everyone enjoyed the work. I noted all the suggestions for improvements so I could enter the corrections on to the computer later.

"Tomorrow we will split up the group," Pak Yarkardin said when we went home in the evening.

"I don't think that is wise," I objected.

"Why not? Then we would make better progress."

I was sure he was right about that. Nevertheless, his suggestion bothered me all night long. If a group were to work independently, how could I ask the right comprehension questions and check that they were not just randomly altering the text and thus straying from the Bible text? It wasn't an option for me but how could I explain that to Pak Yakardin? These questions troubled me and in my mind I could already see that we would fail to achieve our aim. I felt so stressed the next morning. However, in the end, my worries were unnecessary. When I spoke about it openly with Pak Yakardin, he immediately conceded. I was utterly relieved.

We continued our work together with great gusto and made much better progress. We laughed a lot about funny ideas and jokes. Everyone was enjoying this creative work.

"There is actually a better expression for this," Pak Anil, the village elder, said on one occasion. "But I think it would be better not to use it. It is an old expression, which the young people don't understand anymore."

"That is right," I agreed. "We need to make sure everyone can understand it."

Together we searched for good headings for the individual stories. When we read the verses in which Jesus predicted his death and resurrection, someone said, "*Antak ka lemak, nanggung kudai.*" That means, "Before there is joy, there is suffering." Everyone's enthusiastic response spoke for itself. It is a common expression, almost like a proverb, perhaps a little like our "No pain, no gain" and is very relevant to so many situations in our lives. We decided that we would not only take it as the title for the section, but as the title for the whole Gospel.

Right from the start, I was impressed by the enthusiasm, dedication, and perseverance of all those involved, but especially by the tenacity of those farmers, who were not used to sitting down for hours doing concentrated mental work.

Four days later, we really had completed our revision of the entire Gospel. Glad about our achievement, we went our separate ways. It had been worth the effort!

# Chapter 38

# Wild Boar

It was midmorning and I was at home alone. There was a knock at the door. It was a man I didn't know.

"*Ibu*, we have caught a wild boar in a trap. It's quite near the road. Would you like to pick it up by car?"

"How much is it?"

"Only 5000 Rupiah[25]."

"And where exactly is it?"

"Just behind Seram Bulan[26]. I'll come with you and show you."

There were still a lot of wild boar in the forest. The Muslim population, of course, didn't eat pork, but as the pigs often caused a lot of damage in the fields, people set up traps, and at weekends the young lads liked to go hunting for boar with their dogs. Sometimes, the hunters would sell us a boar's leg for 1000 Rupiah and we would have meat for several days. As we didn't have a fridge, which meant the meat went off quickly in the tropical heat, we had to boil it in the morning and evening so that it wouldn't turn sour.

I really didn't need a whole boar, but I knew there were others in our congregation who would enjoy some. I got the car keys and on the way to the garage I let the Pastor, Pak Kor, know. I arrived back half an hour later, and reversed the car up the small path to the pastor's house. Pak Kor had everything ready. The men unloaded the pig, a fully grown male, and carried it to the well. Other helpers were standing around ready with sharpened machetes.

"What bit of the boar do you want?" Pak Kor asked me.

"I would really like a leg, the head and a piece of liver. You can share out the rest."

"You can take the leg straight away."

In no time at all, one of the men had cut off a leg for me. I put it in the back of the car. After lunch I planned to drive to Manna and give it to Ibu Ann who put up some of the school children from the village. I wanted the liver for myself and thought the boar's head would do nicely for my dog and

---

[25]  5000 Rupiah at that time was about 5 DM (roughly £3)
[26]  *Seram Bulan* is the neighbouring village.

her five pups. The puppies were already almost six weeks old and chewed up everything they found between their sharp teeth. Several flip-flops had borne the brunt of those little rascals. Now, they could all have a bone to nibble on.

Half an hour later, there was another knock at my door. One of the men had brought me my order – a lovely bit of liver and the boar's head. I directed him straight to the kitchen area at the back of the house.

"You can put the head in this bowl." It was our washing up bowl. I was horrified when I saw how big the head was. It filled the bowl completely. There was no way that boar's head was going to fit into any of my pans. How was I going to chop it up?

"Can you help me take the head apart?" I asked the man.

Somewhat undecided and hesitant, the man looked at the boar's head and then at me. Probably, he could see my helplessness.

"All right then. Do you have a machete?"

I gave him my big knife.

"But this is totally blunt!" he cried in dismay.

"I'll get you the whet stone," I said quickly, just glad that he had agreed to help me.

He took a long time to sharpen the knife, then he skinned the head and cut off the big ears. The tongue was massive as well. The scrag end filled up the entire wok. Then he opened the skull and took out the brain. Who would eat all that? Perhaps it hadn't been such a good idea to have the head after all.

When he had gone, I had to get it all sorted out before it went off or the flies swarmed all over it, boil up the bones, skin and ears for the dogs in one pan, cut up the liver into slices and quickly fry it, à la my mother's recipe, in the frying pan. The biggest challenge was the rest which I wanted to make into *gulai*[27].

I had never opened a ripe coconut. Even to remove the thick, fibrous outer shell to get to the actual coconut, I found impossible. Nor did I really know what spices and seasonings I needed. I felt quite helpless as I had so little cooking experience. Nenek Em, Sida's mother, was sitting in front of her house and came to my rescue.

I called to her, "Can you help me open a coconut?"

Willingly, she came with me into the kitchen and, in no time at all, she removed the fibrous shell of the coconut and cut the hard inner core in half.

---

[27]  *Gulai* is the name of a meat dish, cooked in coconut milk.

"Thank you so much. I'll scrape it out myself." At least I had learnt how to do that. "But do you think you could tell me what seasoning I need?"

She looked into my spice basket and got out a few onions and cloves of garlic, as well as turmeric, ginger and some other roots. Then she took some coriander, a good handful of chillies and got some lemon grass from the front garden. She crushed them together with rough salt on my stone.

"That should be enough," she said. "Now you can cook your meat."

Satisfied, she left the battle field.

I, too, was satisfied. Who would ever have thought that one day I would learn from the village people how to cook a boar's head?!

# Chapter 39

# Ingenious Car Repairs

Even though our car was only about six years old, it was not in the best state of repair because of the poor road conditions and the climate in southern Sumatra. Again and again, repairs had to be made. I was always very thankful when I arrived safely and without any incident at my destination.

One day I was having to make a necessary trip to Bengkulu. Pak Kor was going with me and there were a few other passengers from the village. As usual, we placed ourselves under God's protection. About half way between Napal Melintang and Bengkulu, I noticed that the car did not feel right. It was hard to steer, and it felt as though it was floating on gentle waves. I stopped by the side of the road to check the tyres. On my side everything seemed in order.

"What's the matter?" Pak Kor's voice sounded a little sleepy.

"Can you check the tyres on your side to see if we have a flat tyre?" I asked him.

He leaned out of the window on his side. "No, the tyres are okay."

"That's strange. Something is not right." With those words I got out and walked around the car to inspect the wheels. No, we really didn't have a flat tyre. But then I saw the problem: the front wheels were not parallel with each other but pointing in different directions.

"Have a look at this," I said to Pak Kor, who had also got out of the car. "There is no way we can drive on."

A passing motorcyclist stopped.

"What's the matter?" he asked.

"The wheels are not lining up," I explained and pointed to the front wheels. "Do you know if there is a garage near here?"

"There's a motorcycle garage in the village," he told us. "They might be able to help you."

A mere 200 metres further on was a small garage – well, that was better than nothing. Carefully, I drove the car over to the garage and the mechanic recognised the problem. "It's the socket joint of the steering that is broken," he explained, "but that's not a problem. We'll just wrap a rubber bandage around it. That will hold, and you will be able to continue your journey to Bengkulu without difficulty."

I felt a little dubious.

He got a long, wide rubber band that had been cut from a car tyre's inner tube and bandaged up the broken joint. Then he wrapped some wire around the bandage. And that was it – the car doctor had done his work. I paid him a meagre sum and thanked him for his good work. The car really did work as normal, just as if nothing had happened. Without any further incidents, we continued safely for another two hours to Bengkulu along a road full of bends and littered with potholes. Probably that ingenious repair would have held good for several hundred more kilometres, but I preferred to take the car to my garage as soon as I could.

I am amazed by the way God works. At the very moment it was needed, help was not far away. Since then I have always carried a big rubber band in my car tool kit. You never know when it might come in handy!

# Chapter 40

# The *Jesus* Film

While I was visiting my American colleagues, Charles and Edna, in Bengkulu, Charles said excitedly, "I now have the *Jesus* film in Indonesian on video." He had bought a television set with a video player and a small generator as well. Equipped with these, he was able to show the film in villages that still did not have electricity.

"Why don't you visit us in Napal Melintang," I suggested. "You haven't been to see us in the village for a while and we could show the film in the church."

We agreed that they would come to visit us at Easter to show the *Jesus* film. (The well-known Jesus film is based on Luke's Gospel and remains quite true to the Bible text.)

A few months earlier I had finished translating the Gospel of Luke into Serawai. After that, it had needed to be thoroughly revised, checked, and corrected. Towards the end of the process, Helen, a consultant from Wycliffe Bible Translators, came over from Jakarta. As she had no understanding of the Serawai language, I had to complete a literal retranslation of the text into English. Helen compared each verse of the text down to the smallest fragment with the original, to make sure that it said the same thing. As well as that, she also asked the local people many questions about their understanding of the text. Sometimes, she had suggestions for improvements, but on the whole, she was satisfied with my work. It was not long before Easter that the revision and corrections had been completed well enough for me to get Luke's Gospel printed off as a small booklet.

As promised, Charles arrived on Good Friday afternoon. As we walked up the slope towards my house, I said, "We shall need to go and see the village head in a little while and we probably ought to set up the equipment in the church before it gets dark." An hour later, when Charles had freshened up and rested a little after his tiring trip, we walked through the village to the house of the village head. He was a Muslim and greeted us warmly. After the formalities, I told him about what we intended to do in the evening.

"My guest has brought a film with him, which he is going to show in the church this evening."

"What kind of film is it, and who is invited?" he asked straight away.

"It is a film about the life of Jesus. It is first and foremost a church event, but of course anyone who wants to see the film can come along. You are also very welcome," I added. He thanked us and offered us the use of the village electricity generator. As it was more powerful than ours, we gladly took him up on the offer. After we left him, we took the equipment to the church and set it up ready for the evening.

When I went back to the church after the evening meal, I could see the stars twinkling in the sky. "Great," I thought to myself. "At least, it should stay dry." When it rained, the rain drops made such a noise on the corrugated iron roof that it was impossible to hear anything. I was just unlocking the church door when Fendi, the son from next door, came up to me. He was studying agriculture in Bengkulu but was home over the Easter weekend.

"Why don't you show the film outside? There is a lot more space," he suggested.

"The equipment is better protected inside and there are benches to sit on," I replied.

"That's true. But outside it would be ideal, wouldn't it? We could set up the television up there on the slope, and the people could sit here on the path or could watch from down there on the street." It was true, the path in front of the church and the village road made a natural arena.

No sooner said, than done. While the men set up the equipment outside, I popped home to get a loudspeaker. It had just occurred to me that we could read out the corresponding texts in Serawai now that we had our brand-new translation, so I collected a few copies of the translated Luke's Gospels and a microphone. When I got back, the first spectators were already there. Soon more and more arrived. As the film began, the spectators squatted down comfortably, both feet firmly on the ground. The village people found that position most comfortable and relaxing and could easily sit for hours that way.

I looked round for Sida. "Sida," I said, "I'd really like to read the texts from Luke's Gospel in Serawai that correspond with the film. You'll help me, won't you?"

The sound of the film was turned down a bit. With the booklet on my knees, the torch in one hand and microphone in the other, I began to read. I soon realised it was not going to be easy to keep an eye on the screen and then quickly find the place again when scenes were skipped. Nevertheless, the spectators enjoyed it.

Sida and I took turns reading. I was concentrating so hard on my reading that I was hardly aware of what was going on around me. Suddenly, I heard a car's horn and saw its headlights. People were becoming restless. It seemed that the village road was full of people who had made themselves comfortable and didn't want to miss any part of the film. Reluctantly, they had to get up to make way for the car. Half an hour later, the car came back the other way and we had the same interruption.

The film was nearing its climax – the suffering of Christ and Jesus' crucifixion – when, suddenly, the spectators began to run off. More and more disappeared. I noticed an unpleasant smell that was becoming more and more pungent.

"That's from a skunk," Sida explained.

None of the spectators stayed until the end of the film.

"Pity," I thought. "At least we'll have another opportunity tomorrow evening."

The following afternoon Fendi came over to see me. "The village head was there last night. He says that we can't show the film in front of our house again, as the crowd blocks the road and makes it dangerous for other people. Instead, he says we should go to the village square and that we are even allowed to use the *hansip*[28] shelter."

"What a good idea. We'll be much less disturbed there." I looked up at the cloudy sky. "Do you think the weather will hold?"

"I think so," Fendi replied confidently. "Oh, and the village head also said that he didn't know you spoke such good Serawai. He was quite moved."

It was nearly dark and there were no stars visible in the sky when we took the equipment to the village square. The *hansip* shelter was a small wooden shelter with big open windows where the village night watchmen sheltered during bad weather. It was on a slope at the edge of the village square, which made it easy for people to see what was happening.

"Lord, please keep the clouds back so that is doesn't rain," I prayed silently. At least, the electric equipment was under shelter.

Once again, a lot of people turned up to see the film. After about an hour, the air began to feel damp. Then there was the occasional raindrop. Slowly, it started to drizzle. At the point in the film where Jesus is arrested and taken to be judged, the rain got stronger and the village square began to empty. We stopped the film when it reached the crucifixion as everyone had gone home. Once more, we were not able to get to the end of the film. What a pity!

---

[28]  The night watchers are called *hansip*.

On Easter Sunday afternoon, we drove to Nanjungan, a village on the coastal road, about twelve kilometres from our village. There, on the oil palm plantation, six to ten Christians, most of them Batak people who worked on the plantation, met regularly for a service. We had announced the film the previous week and they were all looking forward to a change from their usual service.

I didn't have to read out the Serawai translation there as we could use the original sound track with the Indonesian text. Although most of the spectators were Batak from northern Sumatra, we always spoke to them in Indonesian. We sat on mats on the floor and watched intently as the scenes unfolded on the screen. I was looking forward to finally seeing the end of the film. We reached the scenes where Jesus was sentenced, tortured, and making his way to Golgotha when, all of a sudden as the crucifixion scenes were just beginning, there was a quick flicker, and the screen went dark.

"They've turned off the electricity," our host explained. "There's nothing we can do about it." What a disappointment for us all!

The passion of Jesus is often a spiritual battleground, quite possibly evident through the kind of difficulties I have just described. I am glad to say that, in later years, the film was shown several times around Easter on Indonesian national TV.

# Chapter 41

## The Effectiveness of the Bush Telephone

After lunch, once or twice a week, I would drive to Manna, the district town, to go shopping and do other errands. Public offices and the post office officially closed at two o'clock, but office staff members often left their desks half an hour beforehand. In any case, they didn't like it when I took them more work to do just before they were about to go home. As it took about half an hour to drive the twenty kilometres to Manna, I always had to hurry. Whenever I left the village, I would usually take my front door key to the pastor's house in case anything unforeseen happened en route. Not many bush taxis came past our village so I usually gave a lift to people who wanted a ride into town. Often, the ladies wanted to take their produce to sell in the market in Manna.

That day only our trainee student was going with me. We got our errands done in good time and were nearly ready to return home when some men approached me at the front of the market. "Do you still have a couple of free spaces?" they asked. "When are you driving back?"

I didn't know those men. "Where do you want to go?" I asked them.

"We come from Seram Bulan." That was our neighbouring village.

They were pleased to get a free ride and made themselves comfortable on the back seat.

It was just after four o'clock when we set off along the wide main road out of town towards our village. There was hardly any traffic. The road had been newly tarred and there was still a lot of gravel on it. I was just about to slowly overtake a motorbike with two young men on it when the driver, without looking back, cut across me to turn right. The motor bike was side-ways on in front of my car. I slammed on the brakes, but had no chance of avoiding them. In my mind's eye I could already see them both right under my car and tried to steer the car to the side – but the wheels were blocked and wouldn't steer. The handle bars of the motorbike were acting as a brake for the car, and the motorbike was being pushed in a semicircle. I released the brake briefly and managed to steer the car and brought it to a halt at the side of the road.

Normally, in Indonesia, you should not stop when there has been an accident; instead you should drive on to the nearest police station. But I was really unsure and wanted to check on the injured men. I was convinced they would need medical attention. At that moment, a police car stopped next to me so, thankfully, resolving my dilemma. The first thing the policemen did was to check our papers. Mine were all in order. My passengers, however, did not have their ID cards with them. Their details were taken down.

"I am the village head of Seram Bulan," one of the men said.

"In that case you should know that you always have to carry a valid ID card with you," the policeman answered drily.

In the meantime, the other policeman had been looking after the injured motorcyclists. They both had bad grazes and the passenger also had a deep cut which would need stitches. The policemen wanted to see their papers too. The passenger had borrowed the motorbike from his office, so declared himself the driver. Neither of them had a driving licence. When everything had been written down, the policemen took the two men to the hospital while I had to drive to the police station. As a result of the accident, the cooler had been damaged and the water had run out, but it was not too far to drive. My passengers would have to find another ride home.

At the police station, I had to give an account of what had happened, and an accident report was written up. By then it was nearly six o'clock.

"Can I go home now?" I asked. I knew there was little chance of getting a lift back to the village if I had to wait much longer.

"No. We first need to wait for news from the hospital that the two are no longer in danger. One of them could have died."

"What if he has?" I asked, uncertain.

"Then you would have to stay here."

A police officer who was sent to the hospital returned with the good news that the two men were fine. I was dismissed with the proviso that I returned the next morning. "You will have to leave the car you had the accident in here." Well, I could not have driven home with my defective cooler anyway.

It was already dusk when the trainee student and I left the police station with our shopping. The bus station on the opposite side of the road was nearly empty. How were we supposed to get home to the village? There was just one bush taxi still there. I spoke to the driver. "Would you take us to Napal Melintang?"

"No, Bandungayu is the furthest I can take you."

Bandungayu was the village before Napal Melintang and was on a hill. The red mud road from there curved steeply down into the valley.

"Why not?" I asked.

129

"If I am in Napal Melintang and it begins to rain, then there is no way I can get home," he explained.

"I'm sure it is not going to rain," I said, trying to persuade him.

"No, I'll take you to Bandungayu or not at all," he insisted.

It was almost dark and we had no other way of getting home. We would have to walk the last three kilometres or so. The driver stated a fair price which I accepted. When we arrived in Bandungayu, it had started to rain. Neither of us had an umbrella or torch with us so we took cover in the night watch shelter. As soon as the shower was over, we picked up our bits and pieces and started the trek home. The red mud was sodden and stuck to the soles of our shoes, making it difficult to walk. We took off our shoes and carried them in our hands. It was pitch dark and we could hardly see where we were walking. Sharp stones dug into our feet, but we were glad we were able to get home.

As we walked up to our house our *neneks* opened the door. They were overjoyed to see us. They had already heard about the accident and had immediately got the key from the pastor's house, looked after our dogs and cats and locked the hen house. Of course they wanted to know all the details. A few minutes later, Pak Kor arrived at the door. "I am so glad it started to rain, otherwise I would have been on my way to Manna with Pak Jon to visit you in prison."

The next morning, Pak Kor took me to the police station on his motorbike. He stayed with us during the interview with the official and the representative from the office of the injured motorcyclist. An agreement was signed. I was to pay for the damage to the motorbike and my car, and the office of the motorcyclist would pick up the hospital bill for the injured man. It was quite exceptional that I would not have to pay all the costs, because normally it was not the offender who paid but the one who had the money.

# Chapter 42

# Things You Can Eat!

It was around 7 p.m. Wati, the nurse who had taken over the clinic from Renate, and I were busy in the living room when we heard someone opening the gate.

"Open the door!" We recognised the voice of Nenek Wil.

Wati opened the door. Nenek Wini was also there with her friend.

"It's nice of you to call in," I greeted the two ladies.

They got mats from the corner of the room, spread them out in the middle of the floor, and made themselves comfortable. This was their favourite place. Then they opened their little sack which was full of the bits they need for chewing betel nut. With a small knife they cut off a corner of a hard betel nut. They carefully wiped clean a green leaf from a betel pepper plant. They spread a white chalky paste out of a small tub on to it with their fingers. Then they wrapped the piece of betel nut in it along with a bit of chewing tobacco. They popped the whole thing in their mouths and began to chew. They spit their saliva, which had turned blood red, into a tin. Many of the ladies had black teeth from chewing betel nut. It is a mild drug, which acts as a stimulant as well as a relaxant.

"What did you have for your dinner?" Wati asked them.

"*Mbatagh*," they answered tersely.

"What was it you had?" I asked them again. I didn't know the word so I got out my note book and pencil and wrote down the new word. "Tell me what it is."

"They are caterpillars from the coconut tree."

"Can you really eat them?" This was the first time I'd heard about them and wanted to make sure. They assured me that you could. Then Wati asked them if they were the large, pink caterpillars, about the size of a thumb. When the ladies told her they were, Wati got really excited.

"They're so tasty!" she exclaimed, "and they are so expensive. In the market in Medan one caterpillar costs 100 Rupiah. I used to love eating them but we couldn't afford them often. Where did you get them from?"

"We found them on a rotting palm trunk near our rice field," the ladies told her.

"Are there more of them?"

"There are loads."

"May I come and visit you on your field tomorrow? You can show me where the rotting palm trunk is, so I can get some of the caterpillars for myself."

"There's no need for you to come," the ladies said. "We'll bring you some." Wati gladly accepted their offer. Needless to say, I was feeling very curious about all this.

The following evening the two ladies handed Wati a tin full of *mbatagh*. I looked in the tin and saw a mass of big, fat, wriggling caterpillars, some bigger than my middle finger. They were light pink, like cooked prawns, and their heads were dark brown. Wati took them to the kitchen and covered the tin so they couldn't escape.

The next day, just before lunchtime, we had a surprise visit from two young German nurses who had been travelling around the country. They had already visited some of the other islands and had even been to East Timor. Our village was their last stop before they travelled back home to Germany.

I told them we were having something really special for lunch. "It's called *mbatagh*. I've never eaten it before, and it's the first time we've cooked it. *Mbatagh* are caterpillars which feed on rotting coconut trees and, apparently, are very tasty."

The two German girls gulped. Susanne, one of them, told me she had an upset stomach so I suggested she should eat something else and offered her a boiled egg.

"Thank you," she replied. "I'm glad I have an upset stomach."

Wati boiled the caterpillars in salt water, the way she had been taught at home.

"Now you'll have to explain how we eat them," I requested as we sat down for our meal.

"Just put the whole caterpillar in your mouth and bite on it. Then the inside oozes out." She showed us how it was done. "It is so tasty," she assured us.

I plucked up all my courage and followed her instructions. I told myself to shut my eyes and get on with it. At least, I would have tried it then. I put a caterpillar in my mouth. Three pairs of eyes were watching me. I bit, and the inside of the caterpillar flowed into my mouth. To my surprise it really did taste good. It was a little bit sweet but otherwise really difficult to describe. Yes, I enjoyed it so much that I ate another four or five of those delicious caterpillars.

After lunch, as we all drove to Manna to register our guests with the police, the palms of my hands began to itch. I felt like scratching them all the time. Then the soles of my feet began to itch. Two hours later the itching had stopped. That evening, the ladies come over again. They already knew we had visitors.

"They are just like us," they commented brightly, the moment they entered the living room.

"What do you mean, they are just like us?" I felt quite curious.

"Well, they are wearing earrings, just like us," was their intriguing reply.

After we had all made ourselves comfortable on the mat, Nenek Wini asked how we had enjoyed the caterpillars.

"They really are very tasty," I said. "I ate loads. Afterwards, though, I had very itchy hands and feet. Do you think that was related?"

"Quite possible," Nenek Wil replied. "Some people do get an allergic reaction and start itching. I guess you should not eat them anymore."

What a pity! They really were good.

# Chapter 43

# Experimenting with Rat Glue

The barn where Pak Ria, our neighbour, stored his rice was between his house and ours. Every harvest time over the last few years he had stored more rice in it and it was now full to the roof. The family now wanted to turn their stored rice into money so that they could, as had become the trend, build a bungalow out of brick to replace their beautiful wooden house built on pillars. So *Mak*[29] Ria, along with her daughters, had been threshing rice for days. They did this by treading on the rice with their feet until the rice grains came off the ear. The rice was then spread out on mats and dried in the sun, then the husks were removed by a machine in the village. The peeled white rice was then sold at the market.

Little by little the barn, which had been full to the brim, was emptied. The many rats, which had enjoyed a safe existence with easy access to food for years, were forced to find a new refuge. Our roof became their preferred choice. The metal gutters had rusted through in many places and we had repaired the leaky areas by simply sliding new PVA guttering under the old one. This gave the rats an ideal living space where our cats couldn't reach them.

From time to time a rat would fall into the big water container in the bathroom which held the rainwater we used for our daily shower. If the container had water, it was difficult for the rat to get out and it would drown. When that happened, we had to pour all the water away and clean the container. If it was empty, my cat dealt with the rat, but if there was only a little of water left in the basin so that the rat didn't drown, I would have to get it out myself. The cat's fear of water was so much stronger than the draw of a tasty rat.

The rats often organised their racing events in our gutters. What could we do about them? I discussed the different alternatives with the older ladies who came to our house every evening.

"Can you hear the racket those rats are making? Our cats aren't managing to chase them away. What do you think – should I get some rat poison?"

---

[29] *Mak* is the Serawai word for mother. After the birth of their first child, people start being called 'mother of ... '

"No, don't use that," one of the ladies advised. "Your cats might end up dying if they ate a poisoned rat. And if the rats died somewhere out of reach, you would have the smell of rotting rat lingering for days and you wouldn't be able to get rid of it."

"But our cats can't get into the narrow gutters so the rats are enjoying their freedom."

"Apparently you can now get rat glue," another lady told me. "It's a sticky stuff, a bit like glue. You spread it where the rats run and they get stuck."

"And that works?" I decided to try it out.

The next afternoon I bought a tin of rat glue and smeared some of it into a twenty centimetres long section of guttering which would be easy to place into the gutter on the roof. The gutters along the roof of the kitchen area were the easiest to reach. As we did not have a step ladder, I took the rather wobbly washing-up table and put a chair on top of it. Being by far the taller, it was my job to climb up while Wati held the chair steady.

That evening, as we were finishing the washing up from our meal, I remembered the rat glue.

"Let's see if it has been successful already," I suggested to Wati.

We put the table and chair in place and I reminded Wati to make sure she held on to the chair while I climbed up. I reached into the gutter and there, in the glue-smeared piece I had placed in the gutter, there was a big rat. I pulled out the section of guttering and let it drop to the ground. The next moment I noticed our cat greedily eyeing the rat and getting ready to pounce. I feared the worst.

"Wati, take it away!" I called down to her, but she didn't understand what I meant. After all, she was supposed to be holding the chair steady.

Too late! The cat pounced and scooted off with the rat in its mouth and I climbed down from my perch.

It was already getting dark but I could make out our cat which was jumping madly in circles. The rat was glued to the cat's fur! After several attempts, I managed to catch the cat and free it from the rat. The rat was dead and Wati buried it in the front garden. The cat's fur was covered with glue, but it came off quite easily with cooking oil. I forgot about the piece of guttering and left it lying next to the wall.

The next morning, I was sitting with Sida, working on our translation. I could hear so many different sounds – the rattling of crockery in the kitchen, the squawking of the chickens, the singing of a child and the voices of patients in front of our house.

I thought the chickens, and one hen in particular, seemed extremely noisy. She was calling her chicks, whose cheeping seemed to be getting louder and more wretched. After a while she must have gone back to her chicks as they calmed down a little. Then the hen tried calling them again. It went on like that for quite a while which was really quite unusual. Suddenly, it occurred to me what was going on and I jumped up to check. It was as I feared – five little chicks were stuck on the piece of guttering, some only with their feet, but others by their wings as well. A sixth one came running over and immediately got stuck as well. It would have been really funny if it hadn't been so awful. Carefully, I freed the chicks and cleaned their yellow down with oil so they wouldn't get stuck to the mother hen. They look totally dishevelled. Would they survive? It must have been incredibly hot for them having oily feathers, but there was nothing else I could do.

The next morning, when I opened the hen house door, the hen and her chicks came running out. They quickly ran to the nearest blades of grass and greedily drank the dew drops. Although the oil had spread evenly across all ten of the chicks and they no longer looked fluffy, I was relieved to see that otherwise they seemed totally fine.

That was the end of my experiments with rat glue.

# Chapter 44

# Computer Problems

Sida, my translation helper, came every morning and, after a prayer together, we worked at our translation. Apart from her mother tongue, Sida only understood Indonesian so we used the three versions of the Bible in Indonesian as a basis for our translation. I also had a copy of the handbook for Bible translators, which was distributed by the International Bible Society. This clarifies every Bible verse in the original Greek text and offers advice for its translation. Difficulties that could come up in relation to other cultures are highlighted and solutions are suggested. The previous afternoon I had worked through the chapters relevant to the text we were translating that day. Next to the computer I had open another big book: the *Eight Translation New Testament* which has eight English versions at a glance. On the book shelf there were various German versions and Bible commentaries. We were ready to start.

I turned on my laptop. Nothing happened. I tried again. Nothing. That laptop was my second one and had a bigger screen than my first. As we did not have electricity in our village at that time, I ran the computer from a car battery that I charged from a solar panel on the roof. The tools I needed for my work were out of action. What should I do? Should I go back to using pen and paper?

"Let's go back over the texts we did in the last few days," I suggested to Sida. I got out the texts I had already printed out. One of us read the text out loud. Sometimes I would note down alternative words or expressions while we were translating and when we read it over, it soon became obvious which alternatives were better or more fluent. Sometimes Sida would say, "There's a spelling mistake," or "That doesn't sound quite right." Then we would search for a more fluent way. I noted all the corrections with a blue or a red pen. Later, I would need to enter them into the computer.

Another time I remarked, "That sounds very Indonesian. Is there another word in Serawai we could use?" Sida insisted that there was not and held on to her opinion.

Serawai is classed as a middle Malay language. There is a close correlation with Indonesian, which is considered a new Malay language. I searched for an example from daily life in which this word was used and asked Sida how she would express it in Serawai. In that way we sometimes came across a new word which we could use, but often she would simply insist that there was no other word in Serawai.

There were times when I had to go back to the Bible texts and commentaries to gain a better understanding of the text and to get hints on how best to translate it. In that way we would work through the text several times. Finally, we would compare it again with the Bible text to make sure that we had not left out any phrases or words. Even if we were convinced ourselves that our translation was good, it was later discussed sentence by sentence with the elders. The point of that was mainly to check comprehension and the natural flow of the language.

We made good progress and carried on until lunchtime. Then it was the weekend. On the Monday we started work again. After a time of prayer, but still feeling slightly tense, I turned on the computer. Hallelujah! It was working so we could continue working at our translation. About two weeks later it happened again. Nothing happened when I pressed the button. Despite praying, it was the same again the next day.

"No, I am not going to be defeated!" That was my decision. Whatever the situation, we would carry on with our work. "Lord, help us!" we prayed. "Show us what is going on here."

When nothing happened again the next day, I reached for pencil and paper.

"I think my computer is broken," I said to Wati, who was living with me in the house. "I desperately need to get it repaired. Either I have to take it to Jakarta myself, which is of course time consuming and expensive. Or I send it to Jakarta and hope that I will get it back in one piece."

I decided on the second option. In Manna I bought a piece of plastic foam, three centimetres thick, wrapped the computer in it to protect it, added a letter of explanation, and sent the parcel by express delivery to Jakarta. My prayers went with it. About ten days later my parcel arrived back. I opened it expectantly. What had had to be repaired? How much had the repair cost? There was neither bill nor letter in the parcel. Was the repair still covered by the guarantee? Fine by me. I was glad to have my computer back so I could continue working on it.

A few weeks later the same thing happened again – the computer wouldn't turn on. The following day, it worked again as if nothing was wrong. This happened at regular intervals. Every morning we experienced the same tension: would the computer cooperate or would it let us down? And then it got to a point where it failed to function for several days in a row.

I decided to send it to Jakarta again. Once again, I received neither bill nor explanation on its return. We always prayed for protection, even for our technical equipment. We knew our battle is not against flesh and blood, but against the powers and authorities in the unseen world. Even though I felt a stab in the pit of my stomach every time the computer didn't work and I had to change my plans, I was determined I was not going to be influenced by it. "Lord, you are bigger than this. To you is given all power and authority, in heaven and on earth, even over computers!"

Nevertheless, the same thing happened again a few weeks later. Some days the computer failed but the next day it would be working normally. Then it would stop working again for several days on end.

The time came when I had to go to Java for a conference and would be travelling through Jakarta. I decided to plan an extra day there so that I could take the computer to the repair shop myself and talk to the technician. The technician greeted me warmly. He remembered when I told him I had sent my laptop to him twice to get it repaired.

"The same problem comes up again and again," I explained, while I unpacked the laptop. He plugged it in.

"Now look at this," I said as I turned it on. To my amazement, the screen lit up.

"It's working again," I exclaimed in surprise. "Back home it wasn't working at all. Could you tell me what you did to repair it?"

"I didn't do anything. It always worked here, just as it has right now," he explained, "so I've always sent it back."

I felt like an ignorant little girl.

I was perplexed and explained how I ran the computer using my solar panel and the car battery.

"The electricity supply goes via the cable, bypassing the rechargeable battery and so the electricity goes directly into the electronics," he explained. "It would seem that your computer isn't coping with that."

I packed up my computer and said goodbye. At the checkout, I ordered a spare rechargeable battery and a charger. I decided that in future I would run the computer only via the rechargeable battery which I could recharge using the charger I run from my solar panel system. After that I didn't have any more computer problems.

# Chapter 45

# The Calendar Campaign

"I'd like to get some scripture verses printed onto calendars with Bible pictures. Is that possible?"

I was in the printing shop of Pak Yohannes, a Chinese Christian man, who had already printed some booklets for me in Serawai.

"Yes, of course it's possible," he assured me.

In Indonesia, many shops and businesses gave their regular clients a large wall calendar at the end of the year, as a sort of advertising gift. Each calendar page normally contained the name of the business or the shop in big print. In previous years, Renate had sometimes given away calendars with Bible pictures at the clinic, but without advertising the clinic. At that time, she got the Christian bookshop in Surabaya to supply the calendars. Those calendars were very popular in the villages as they were often the only calendar a family owned. The pictures frequently remained on the wall as a decoration for years. I wanted to give away calendars with Bible pictures and a verse from the Bible. I could imagine this Bible verse being read by all visitors for many years to come.

Pak Yohannes got out a thick advertising book. "There are pictures here of all the calendars on the market for the coming year. Have a look through it. You are sure to find something you like, although there is always the possibility that certain calendars have already been sold out." I hadn't expected that as it was only September.

I leafed through the catalogue. There were all sorts of calendars with many different pictures – flowers, animals, ladies and scenery as well as abstract images. Right at the back there were calendars with religious images from Islam, Buddhism, Hinduism and also Christianity. I didn't like some of the pictures of angels but there were some good illustrations of stories from the Gospels, exactly in line with what I had in mind. I chose two different calendars and asked for 50 of each adding that if one of them was already sold out, then I'd have 100 of the other one.

"What would you like to have printed on them?" Pak Johannes asked.

"I would like to have a Bible verses in Serawai in the space where you would normally put the address. That would be possible, wouldn't it?"

"Yes of course. We can print anything."

"Would it be possible, then, to print a different Bible verse on each page, one that fits in with the story?"

"No, I'm sorry but that's not possible. It has to be the same on each page."

I felt a little disappointed. "That's a pity. Let me have a good think about which verse to put on."

Pak Johannes suggested that he should order the calendars before I decided what should be printed on them. He assured me that if they were still available he should receive them within two or three weeks. That suited me fine.

"Do I need to pay a deposit?"

"No, that's not necessary. Let's see if the calendars are available first."

When I returned in October, Pak Yohannes was not in town. I talked with one of his members of staff who told me the calendars had arrived.

"Great. I have brought the Bible verse I want printed on them."

"Which name and address would you like to put below it?"

"Under no circumstances do I want my name and address on it, just the Bible verse."

"We could print it a little bit smaller."

"No, please don't. I just want the Bible verse, nothing more," I stressed.

It must have seemed very unusual to the man that someone wanted to give away calendars without using it as an advertising tool for himself or his business. However, he still insisted on taking my name and address so that he knew who had placed the order. We discussed the font and the colour of the text. I had to entrust the rest of the graphic layout to the printer as I lived too far away to be able to pop in easily to have a look. I hoped that he would do a good job. After all, he had had a lot of experience.

At the end of November, I went into the printers again. This time Pak Yohannes was there and confirmed that my calendars were ready. He went off to fetch samples.

A few moments later, he returned and handed me a copy of each of the two calendars I had ordered. Under the Bible verse, clearly visible was my name and address. I was horrified.

"I expressly said that I only wanted the Bible verse printed in big letters on these calendars," I protested.

"But it doesn't really matter, does it, that your name is on it? The verse is still obvious enough," he said, trying to calm me down.

I shook my head. "But I don't want my name displayed in houses all over the area. Can't you take it off again?" I asked in despair.

"That's tricky. The colour is too bright. If you cover it with white, it will still shine through."

"Just try, please. There is no way I can take the calendars like this. There is still time until the end of the year. I'll come back before Christmas."

"Okay then," he said. "We'll try. But you'll still be able to see it a little because the colour is so strong."

"That wouldn't be as bad as displaying my name and address."

I felt somewhat relieved and hopeful that there would be an acceptable solution to the problem. I thanked Pak Yohannes and took the two messed up copies with me. One of them I later gave to our pastor.

When I went to see Pak Yohannes again just before Christmas, the calendars were still not ready. He said he had had a lot to do and promised me he would attend to them as soon as he could. Pity. I would have liked to have had them to give as Christmas presents to members of the congregation and some other acquaintances. I consoled myself with the thought that you can still give calendars away in January.

But in January the calendars were still not ready. I was beginning to feel impatient. At the beginning of February, I was in Bengkulu again. The calendars were still not ready and Pak Yohannes was in Jakarta to celebrate Chinese New Year. I was frustrated. There seemed no point in giving away calendars in the middle of the year.

In March, just before Easter, I knocked on Pak Yohannes' door once more.

"Are my calendars ready yet?" I asked.

There was a slightly incredulously look on his face.

"I've had them sold off cheaply in the market," he confessed. "I didn't think you would still want them. I got rid of them easily enough."

I was lost for words. The thought that my name and address would be displayed in one hundred houses for all to see took some getting used to. I felt exposed and put on show, but there was nothing I could do about it.

My calendar with the Serawai Bible verse and my name and my address hung in the entrance room at our pastor's house. Each time I went to his house for a meeting, I saw it on the wall and was reminded of the other ninety eight calendars that were hanging up somewhere on people's walls, people I didn't even know. And every time a feeling of dread came over me.

It was the middle of the year, and once again I was sitting opposite my calendar during a prayer meeting and looked up at it. This time the Bible verse caught my eye and it was as though God was speaking to me, "My word is displayed in a hundred homes in which most of the people don't know me. And it didn't even cost you a single Rupiah. Just be happy about that."

Part 4

# Project Closure

# Chapter 46

# A Different Kind of Language Test

As I was working under the sponsorship of the Indonesian Missionary Fellowship, it was the principal of the Bible School in Tanjung Enim[30] , on the other side of the Barisan mountain range who was responsible for me with regards to the authorities. It was he who had to sign my annual application for my visa extension at both the police station and the immigration office, so at least once a year, and whenever possible to coincide with the Bible students' graduation or commissioning, I would travel there for a visit.

I loved those journeys over the mountains to Tanjung Enim. During those long, mostly 12-hour trips, all sorts of memories came flooding back. Sometimes Renate and I travelled overnight by car. The journey took us from Bengkulu up into the mountains and then through the mountain valley to Pagar Alam. From there, we would drive down the other side of the Barisan range over Lahat and Muara Enim until we reached Tanjung Enim. At times the road was so full of pot holes that we could only creep forward at a snail's pace. Sometimes it seemed that we drove out of two holes only to drive into three new ones.

One day we decided to take the longer route which took us much less time. This road took us via Curup and Lubbuk Linggau to the Transsumatra Highway on the other side of the mountains. We then travelled south on this highway which was really quite narrow. It was much used by lorries and buses, and sometimes when a big lorry came towards us we had to veer out of the way, even with one wheel off the road, in order not to have an accident. That was why we usually decided to make the journey over the mountains to Pagar Alam which, although it was a significantly shorter route, was no quicker but much more adventurous.

When I had to travel to Tanjung Enim on my own, I liked to go on the public bus. The bus I normally travelled on was the one to Jakarta. It left Bengkulu in the early afternoon, travelled over Curup and joined the highway at Lubbuk Linggau. This meant I arrived in Tanjung Enim sometime

---

[30]  The *Indonesian Missionary Fellowship* run a Bible school in Batu, East Java, as well as one in Tanjung Enim, South Sumatra.

between two and four o'clock in the morning. I would get off at the police station and the guard there would phone the Bible School for someone to come and pick me up. If that didn't work because nobody answered the phone, I had to take a *becak*[31] or a policeman might take me to the Bible School by motorbike.

Because of the unsociable time of arrival of this night bus, I decided to try the daytime bus which went from Bengkulu via Pagar Alam. I made enquiries at the bus station about departure times a few days before I was due to travel and received conflicting information. I came to the conclusion that the first bus most probably left between seven and eight o'clock in the morning.

I arrived there early and got a good seat but it was a good while before the bus was just about full. It was one of the small, narrow buses that are better able to negotiate the narrow curves of the road. The journey into the mountains began. All along the way there were people waiting to get on, most of them with a lot of luggage which was stowed on the roof. After a good two hours we arrived in Kepahiang up in the mountains. From there we drove through a mountain valley on a slightly narrower road southwards towards Pagar Alam. Although the air up in the mountains was considerably cooler, I was getting thirsty. It was then that I realised that I had forgotten to take anything with me to eat or drink. I was sure we would take a break, at least I hoped we would. But the bus drove on.

The River Musi rises there in the mountains and later flows through the great plain in the east. By the time it reaches Palembang, it is several hundred metres wide. For a long time we drove along by the side of the river, which at that point was still quite narrow. The surrounding hills were ideal for coffee plantations. We drove past handsome wooden houses whose carved veranda railings and colourful glass windows with floral designs indicated the wealth of their owners. Some houses had a huge front yard on which coffee was spread out to dry. There were villages all along the road and it was not always clear where one village ended and the next began. Eventually, the bus driver stopped for a rest in a small town, but there was no restaurant and no toilet. We didn't stop for long!

It was after one o'clock when we finally reached Pagar Alam. I felt quite dehydrated and had a headache. I had hardly got off the bus when several men pounced on me, shouting, "Tourist! Tourist!" and tried to relieve me of my bag. I held on to it with both hands.

---

[31] *Becak* is a rickshaw-like bike taxi, where the passenger sits on a seat in front of the cyclist.

"Where do you want to go?" they asked.

"I want the bus to Lahat."

"We'll take you there." Once again they tried to take my bag. "The bus is already waiting two roads further on."

"I'll make my own way, thank you," I said, declining their offer. Two of them turned towards easier targets.

"No, I'll take you," another one insisted, walking along by my side.

I didn't know how to defend myself. Then it occurred to me that the local people sometimes just got angry. I decided to try that and went for it. "I am not a tourist. Leave me alone. I can find the bus myself. And anyway, I am not feeling well, and I have a headache, and ... ." I ran out of words. I had spoken in Serawai which is not that different from the Pasemah spoken here in Pagar Alam.

I was not really convinced that that was the right way to act as a Christian. On the other hand, I noticed a curious change in the young man. Suddenly, he became friendly and helpful. By that time, however, we had arrived at the waiting buses. There, too, several men jumped towards me and wanted to pull me towards their bus. Somehow, I managed to fend them off and picked my own bus which was not yet full.

"How long until you leave?" I asked.

"We'll be leaving soon," came the reply.

"I'd really like to get something to eat at that inn over there."

"You can't. We are about to leave."

"Let me just go and buy something," I insisted and walked over to the restaurant. I ordered a noodle dish with lots of broth, but before they managed to serve it I was called back to the bus. "Hurry up, we are about to leave!"

"Could you wrap the noodles up for me?" I asked.

With my noodle soup in a little plastic bag, I sat down in the bus. My seat was right next to the exit. The young men came over straight away.

"How come you know our language?" they demanded.

"I live in Pino."

They were still not convinced that I really was able to speak their language and they asked me lots of questions, which I answered, much to their satisfaction. One of them came over with a piece of bamboo, with a small opening, a sort of water bottle used a lot in the villages.

"Do you know what this is?" He held the bamboo receptacle in my face.

"That is a *gerguak*," I said confidently.

"She knows it, she really does," he shouted and jumped away happily.

In a flash, the atmosphere changed dramatically and the men bent over backwards to be polite. One of the men, noticing my desperate attempts to eat noodle broth out of a plastic bag without a spoon, brought me a bowl and a spoon. "Take this. That will make it easier."

I ate my soup before the bus left, while the men stood in front of the open door and watched me benevolently.

It would appear that I had passed the language test and had been accepted as one of them.

# Chapter 47

# Stolen Papers, but no Body

Once again I had to go to Bengkulu for some errands and a handful of people had asked me for a lift. Our Pastor, Pak Kor – who has since been transferred – asked me to get him some seedlings for his coffee field near to Bengkulu. He also needed a few other items relating to his move.

"The road to Bitungan is now passable by car," he assured me. "It will only be a small detour for you." With that in mind, I agreed to take him and the things he wanted up to his house in his coffee garden.

A few other people from the village also wanted a lift to Padang Capau up in the mountains. Of course, all of them had luggage so my car was fully loaded and all seats were taken. Nenek Umir, one of the grandmothers, was visiting in the mountains for the first time and was sitting next to me. I asked her to hold my hand bag on her lap.

Those who wanted to go up into the mountains got out at the turning at Suka Raja and waited there for a vehicle for the next leg of their journey. Only Pak Kor, his wife and their three children were left in the car. After about 30 kilometres, we reached to the turning to Bitungan. The red mud path was dry and passable; the conditions seemed fine and we should have no difficulty in reaching our destination. Then we got to a stream, over which there was a small bridge, really only designed for motorbikes. Pak Kor got out and inspected the situation.

"What do you think?" I called out to him.

"There is nothing we can do," he answered resignedly. "I can't see any tyre tracks and the bank is too steep."

I got out and had a look. He was right. There was no way I was going to get across the bridge with the car or through the water.

"What shall we do now? Do you want to come with me to Bengkulu and go to your field from there?"

"No, we won't make it today. We are not far away here. Over there is a house. We could ask them to take care of our things and then we'll carry them to our hut from there."

So we all got out and began to unload the things from the car. At that moment, two young men on a motorbike came by. They got off and started a conversation with us. Pak Kor asked them if there was another way but it seemed there wasn't. Suddenly, I remembered that my handbag was lying on the front seat of the car which had its windows wide open. I glanced in the car and noted with relief that it was still there. Shortly afterwards, the two men took their leave very quickly and zoomed off rather fast on their motorbike.

We unloaded the rest of Family Kor's belongings and I said goodbye. When I arrived in Bengkulu, at the home of Pastor Dandra, I discovered that my purse, which contained my various important documents, such as my immigration card and my driving licence, was missing. It had been in the bag, of that I was quite certain.

Had Nenek Umir taken them during the long journey? I really could not imagine that she would have done that. In any case, it would have been too obvious and our suspicions would have pointed immediately to her. But who else could have done that? One of the young men on the motorbike? Even that I considered unlikely. The bag lay in the middle of the car after all. I had no obvious explanation.

The next day, I went to the immigration office to report my lost ID card.

"That is serious," they warned me. "Without the ID card you can't have your visa extended."

"And what do I need to be able to apply for a new ID card?"

"First we need the police to certify that the ID card has been lost. Before that we can't do anything."

When I arrived back at home in the village, I drove to the police station in Manna to report the loss of my purse containing my papers. I received the certification I requested, listing the entire contents of my purse. I also needed a new driving licence. As the ID card with the code of my finger prints was also in the purse, I first had to provide the prints of all ten of my fingers again before I could receive a new licence.

Two weeks later I drove to Bengkulu again. I urgently needed to apply for a new immigration card as my visa was running out. I got out at Pastor Dandra's house.

"Here comes the body!" Pastor Dandra greeted me excitedly.

"What do you mean?" I looked at him bemused. He handed me an envelope.

"Are these not your missing papers?"

I looked at them carefully. They were most definitely my papers, and they were all there: Personal ID card, immigration card, driving licence and the card with my finger prints on it. Even the photo of my niece, which I always carry in my purse, was still there. People often asked me whether that beautiful girl was my daughter. Usually, I just smiled. The photo had become somewhat bumpy with moisture but my documents were laminated and had remained undamaged.

"How did they get here?" I asked, hardly able to believe my eyes.

"A man from the congregation brought them to me. He came to me and asked, 'Isn't this the missionary who comes and sees you from time to time?' I wanted to know where he got this from. He told me he found it scattered by the side of the road. He searched all around the forest, but didn't find any body."

It appeared that the men had only taken the money and the telephone card and had simply thrown the rest away. I was so thankful that I could save myself the hassle of going to all the various offices to get new papers.

Even today, I have two cards containing the code of my fingerprints – interestingly two different sets. The codes for the fingerprints do not match. Not one single finger matches! You would hardly be able to use them to identify my body.

# Chapter 48

# God's Angels are Active

Every time I completed the translation of a portion of the Bible, I felt like celebrating. I allowed myself a day off, invited my Indonesian co-worker and the young people from our congregation to accompany me, and we would drive to the coast for a day at the beach.

That particular day was a very special day: the draft translation of the New Testament into Serawai was finished. There were still lots of corrections to be done, it still needed to be checked and revised, but a big milestone had been reached.

The others were all excited. My translation helper, Sida, the two young girls, Yal and El, who helped me run the household during their summer holidays, and the nurse, Wati, were all busy getting the next day's picnic ready. I donated a chicken, which needed to be killed, plucked and cooked in coconut milk. It would be accompanied by rice and vegetables. The rice would be boiled early in the morning. Fresh banana leaves were collected and passed over the fire to smooth them out. They would be used to wrap up the hot rice and later, during they picnic, they would serve as environmentally friendly disposable plates. A few canisters of drinking water, bananas and other fruit were got ready, as well as pamphlets to give away and, last but not least, our swimming things.

It was a short night. At four o'clock, I heard the girls busy in the kitchen, cooking the rice. We wanted to set off at dawn, around half past five. Though the beach at Linau was no more than 150 kilometres away, the road was generally in poor condition and in parts was quite narrow, with many bends, so we had to count on four to five hours driving time. The cargo area at the back of my pickup, a Toyota Kijang, had a roof, and there were cushioned benches on either side.

When I got the car out of the garage, the other passengers appeared. As well as those already mentioned, Pak Legimin, our young Javanese preacher, Ibu Ann, an older Timorese colleague from Manna, and perhaps another eight young people were going with us. Before setting off, we prayed and committed ourselves into God's care for the day. It was a cheerful, expectant crowd that set off in the early morning. The tarpaulins on either side of the back of the pickup were still down to keep the chilly morning air out. There was not much space at the back and, after about an hour's drive, we got the first complaints, "The car is so uncomfortable; the exhaust fumes are coming in. Why don't you have a better car?" I asked myself why the whingers even bothered coming along. I hadn't made them come; they had chosen to come on an adventure. I stopped and we rolled up the tarpaulins, but that didn't stop the complaining. There were too many pot holes for that. Neither could the passengers at the back see a lot of the fascinating scenery, the rickety bridges over deep ravines, and the extensive rice fields in the valleys, the palm groves and the coffee and clove gardens.

At the side of the road, I notice a monkey family: Daddy and Mummy monkey, with Baby monkey sitting comfortably on a tree. Three monkey children were jumping around on the telephone cables along the road. Like tight rope walkers, they were trying to walk upright along the cable, but kept falling off. Cleverly, they hung from the cable and swung themselves up again to have another go. I had to look twice, wondering if I saw correctly. The monkeys didn't seem to have a problem keeping up with progress.

After about four hours' drive we finally arrived in Bintuan, the district town in southern Bengkulu. Our destination, the beach at Linau, was barely half an hour away. Just a few more bridges to cross, a hill to drive around and, suddenly, the bay with its blue sea and golden sand beach lay before us. What a sight for sore eyes!

Yes, the long drive and the immense effort really had been worth it. It was going to be a lovely day. This bay is a natural port and a boat sails from it to Enggano Island every couple of weeks. Some fishing boats were hauled up onto the sandy shore. The waves were breaking on the sand, the foam rolling up the beach. What a beautiful scene!

Before going for a dip in the sea, we drove on a few more kilometres to the next bay which we had discovered during a previous visit. There, a big rock jutted out into the surf, like the prow of a ship riding the waves. The beach was wide and lined with palm trees. There we rested, sang together and listened to God's word. The wind was blowing the sand into our faces, but that didn't stop us. I had taken the Gospel of Luke in Serawai with me, and together we read Chapter 18, verses 15 to 17. That was the Bible text given for the day. We thought especially about verse 17, "Unless you become like children, you cannot enter the Kingdom of God." Using questions, I tried to unpack the meaning of the text. What did Jesus mean when he said we should become like children in order to be able to enter the Kingdom of God? We shared our thoughts and came to the agreement that it was all about the unshakable trust a child has in his father. What does our trust in God look like? How can we put it into practice? I had the impression that this Bible text was speaking to a few of the young people in particular, but I did not want to draw out our time of sharing. We ended with a prayer and a song.

Now it was time for our picnic and I was certainly ready for my lunch! The food we had brought was enough for everyone. Afterwards, we went for a stroll along the beach. It was not long before we headed back to the first bay, as the water babies amongst us had been looking forward to a swim in the sea for days. There were no rocks in the bay and the beach dropped away rather quickly. Once past the first breaker, the water was deep enough to swim in.

I had put on my swimming costume under my shorts and T-shirt and, together with Wati, I approached the surf. The waves were surprisingly strong and rolled all the way up the beach. Yal and El also got changed, but Pak Legimin, who was usually the first in the water, didn't seem keen on going in. I watched the waves for a bit. When a wave broke, the aim was to throw ourselves into the water as quickly as possible in order to get behind the next big breaker before it rose up and broke. We started running, but did not quite manage it, and the wave washed us several metres up onto the beach. We tried again and this time it worked. Soon, Yal and El were also with us in the water.

That day, however, swimming in the sea was somehow not much fun. The water was very choppy which meant it took a lot of energy to swim. I was just wondering whether we should not be getting back to shore when Yal pointed to the beach. Several people were running agitatedly around and pointing to the water. Yal was the first to see Lena. Lena had tried to come into the water after us, but had been knocked over by a wave and had got into difficulties. The strong current was dragging her away. Yal and El wanted to swim over to her, but I whistled at them to get back. "Everyone get out of the water!"

Those on the beach had already noticed what was happening. The men ran over to help. I knew they would watch and wait if they saw us rushing over to help her. But none of us had lifesaving experience and we were struggling against the waves ourselves. Yet I asked myself whether I should attempt to swim out to her. But what if Lena, in her panic, held on to me and we both went under, and the whole group was stranded? No, I couldn't risk it.

When we got back on shore, I could see that even the local men were not daring to go into the surf. Should we have dared after all? The young people from our village were running around the beach in desperation and had started the death lament. Even Ibu Ann and Pak Legimin were running around in a daze.

"Stop screaming and pray!" I shouted to the young people and that indeed was what they did. They sat down on the sand in twos and threes and began to pray.

I grabbed Ibu Ann, and together we called out to God for help. At the same time I kept an eye on what was happening on the beach. A man had got hold of a large canister although he still did not dare to get in the water as Lena was still being pulled away by the current. It seemed so hopeless. As we prayed on the beach, the situation changed unexpectedly. As though by an invisible hand, a wave brought Lena closer to the beach. The man with the canister plucked up the courage to get into the water and managed to grab her. Others rushed over to help him. Wati was there at once. They turned Lena upside down and Wati started pumping on her stomach. As she was doing so, she repeated again and again, "Dalam nama Yesus!" ("In the name of Jesus!"). For myself, I had no idea of what kind of first aid was required after a bathing accident. All I could see was that Lena's body was completely stiff and almost black and that nothing was happening.

"Oh God, help! Let her come round again!"

"Take her to the doctor's!" a few people suggested when, after a while, still nothing had happened.

"Where is the nearest doctor?" I asked.

"In Bintuan," they replied. That was nearly half an hour's drive away.

All I could think was, "If she is not breathing now, how is she going to start breathing in half an hour's time when we are at the doctor's?"

I did not say anything but obediently sat down at the steering wheel, wet as I was and covered in sand. The people lifted the cushioned seating off the benches and placed it on the floor of the cargo area of the car, ready to lay Lena on it. I could hear some people on the beach asking, "Who is this Jesus you keep talking about?" But I didn't have the time right then to explain it to them.

I had just started the engine when there was a knock from the back. "Wait a minute. She has just coughed out some water," a voice called.

Unconvinced, I got out again and checked for myself. She was coughing out even more water. It was true! She really had come back to life. We were all incredibly relieved. "Thank you Lord, for this miracle."

Nevertheless, we packed everything up as quickly as we could and drove to Bintuan to see the doctor. When we found him, and I was reassured that Lena was in good hands, I showered and got changed.

I was immensely grateful for God's intervention. I could not imagine what would have happened if I had got back to the village with a dead body. Presumably, I would have had to leave the village at once. For days afterwards, I still trembled inwardly when I thought about the situation. It had been rather reckless of me not to take better note of the waves. The way the surf was, we really should not have gone in the sea at all that day. And I had never asked Lena if she could swim. I had no idea that she had never bathed in the sea and did not know the power of the waves.

After an hour of waiting and resting in Bintuan, we began our long journey home. Lena was lying on the cushioned seating in the back of the car. I had four girls sitting next to me on the front bench, and everyone else was sitting on the iron rods on which the cushioned seats would normally be. No-one complained about the uncomfortable ride. They were all so thankful and glad that God had answered our prayers and Lena was alive.

# Chapter 49

# Curious Logic

"Here are some more of those bamboo arrows again!"

Wati picked up several arrows that were lying on the ground in our front yard and threw them over the fence.

We had just returned from a shopping trip to Manna. We had walked up the path together and I followed Wati through our gate.

"What do you mean 'again'?" I asked. "Has this happened before?"

"Yes, every time we've been out and come back home, there were arrows here in the front yard. I've always got rid of them, which is why you have never seen them because you were usually still putting the car in the garage."

Who was throwing those arrows into our property and what for? It was a mystery to us. Were they destined for our dogs? From time to time I had found unusual wounds on them, which were definitely not from fighting with other animals. Our two dogs Putih and Blacky were, like all of the dogs in the village, local mongrels. But as we fed them regularly and mixed a bit of dried, salted fish into their rice, they were bigger and stronger than most of their contemporaries in the village. They were, in a way, the leaders of the village pack. Browny, our young female dog, was still very playful, but appeared strong and brave when she was with her two big "brothers". The village lads always got annoyed when, as they passed our house on their way to their fields or on their way home, our dogs barked and chased after their dogs. They would often take a detour. But would they consider that a reason for attacking my dogs so viciously? The lads had always enjoyed taking our dogs hunting for wild boar and would leave us a small share of the spoils as reward.

But if it was not our dogs that were the target, who or what was? Were the arrows designed for Wati, who had been running the clinic for the last few years, or Inik, the young girl from the neighbouring village who helped us around the house and had recently started living with us? Had she got a bit too friendly with one of those young men? Or were the arrows possibly meant for me? But if so, why? What was going on? We had no explanation, but kept an ear open.

I was quite worried about the safety of my house mates. That evening, I went to see the village head, Pak Wil, to inform him of these goings-on. One of the village teachers was also there for a visit. He told me that the evening before he had overheard my neighbour's lad Ruben boast to his friends that he had tied Blacky, one of my dogs, to a tree and had abused him. The village teacher, standing in the shadow of a tree, had not been seen in the dark. At that time many of the young people were not able to find any work after they left school. They came back to the village, quickly became bored and started to get silly ideas. Ruben was the oldest of them and one of their leaders. He was also one of those leading the youth at church.

The next day Wati came across a further piece to our puzzle. The little boy of one of our neighbours had run home, shouting, "Mummy, Mummy, Ruben has killed and eaten one of Ibu Hildegard's chickens."

"Shush, child, don't shout so loudly, otherwise Ruben will kill you too," the mother cautioned as she tried to calm the boy.

At least, we now knew why one of our cockerels had disappeared a few days earlier.

A few days later, I was out in the car with a few of the teenagers. Ruben, by far the oldest, was sitting in the front. On the way home I stopped in Kelutum to get something from one of the shops, leaving the passengers in the car. While I was away, Ruben searched the car, found a bit of loose change that I kept for car parking, took it and bought two cigarettes with it. I only found out about it from the others when we were back at home. What made me most cross about the whole thing was that he did it in front of the younger children. As a youth leader he should have been setting an example!

We knew that situation must not be allowed to continue. But how were we to find him out? What was the appropriate action in this society? Should I go to the village elder or to a relative? I decided to talk to Pak Ipi about it. He was the oldest of Ruben's cousins.

The very next evening, I went to the family's house. Pak Ipi was at home but so were his wife and children. I should have thought about that. Would that really be the right time to voice my concerns? After a while I came out with it after all.

"Pak Ipi, what would you advise your daughter to do if she was away from home and wrote to you that her dog was being abused, mysterious arrows were lying in front of her house, and chickens and money were being stolen?"

He answered promptly, "I would tell her, 'It's not safe there. Come home at once.'"

158

Well, that was not really what I wanted to hear. Feeling a little bewildered, I remained silent.

"Has something like that happened?" he asked.

And so we started talking about my observations. I was close to tears. The last thing I wanted to do was leave the village now that the translation project was nearly finished. He promised to look into the matter and to report it to Pak Anil, the village elder.

Two days later, after sunset, there was a knock at my door. It was Ruben.

"I want to talk to you," he said. We sat down. "Pak Ipi told me that various unexplained things are happening in your house."

"That's right."

"Well, I didn't have anything to do with any of it."

"But do you know, perhaps, who is behind it all?"

"No, I don't."

The conversation was not getting us anywhere and I was wondering why he had come.

I apologised and said, "I am sorry if I wrongly suspected you."

As he left, he turned to me, took my hand, and said, "I am sorry."

Then he ran off as fast as he could. I remained standing at the door, nonplussed.

At that moment, Pak Anil walked through the gate. He had witnessed the last scene. When we sat down, he asked, "Did Ruben apologise?"

"He denied it all. But just now, as he was saying goodbye, he grabbed my hand and said, 'I am sorry.' What was that all about?"

"So he did admit everything," he replied.

The logic of that was too complicated for me. Unfortunately, we were not able to continue talking about it because some of the other men arrived for a meeting to help revise and correct the translated Bible text. However, I resolved to have a prayer evening soon to pray for the young people in our village.

Sadly, that was not the end of the saga with Ruben.

# Chapter 50

# God's Ways are Different

The front door opened. It was almost nine o'clock and was pitch dark outside. Wati had been at the children's club. She came in, totally out of breath.

"What is going on?" I asked her.

I was sitting at the table with Pak Anil and two of the church elders for our weekly meeting to revise the translated texts. There had been a big storm earlier and so only a few had come to that evening's meeting.

"That's the last straw!" Wati burst out. "Let me tell you all about it." You could feel her agitation.

Wati is a Batak girl from Medan in northern Sumatra. Her father had a high rank in the military. She has six brothers and two sisters. The family used to live on military property and, as a child, she joined her brothers playing tricks on the new soldiers, so she was used to quite a bit.

"Ruben threatened me with a knife."

Four pairs of eyes were looking at her.

"How did that happen? Tell us."

"Well, earlier there was the storm, wasn't there?" She was seething. "We had just finished the children's club so I quickly ran next door to the pastor's house to shelter and didn't lock the door of the church straight away. Then the church bells started ringing. Didn't you hear them?" We hadn't, as the drumming of the rain on our corrugated iron roof had drowned out any other sound.

"I went outside and shouted to one of the girls standing in front of the church door, 'Shut the door.' Then I got the key to lock up. At that point, the door was kicked open from the inside. Ruben was standing there with a Muslim friend. 'What are you doing here?' I asked him. 'We were ringing the church bells,' he answered rudely. 'You can't do that,' I told them. 'Anyway, we are locking up now. Off you go.' He didn't like that. He grabbed a knife out of his friend's trouser pocket and threatened me. 'Are you bringing a Muslim into church to cause trouble here?' I calmly admonished him. That made him even angrier. His friend quickly took the knife off him. I stayed very calm. But when I think about it now, it really was quite frightening."

We all agreed with her and encouraged her to report it to the village head in the morning. After breakfast the next day, Wati left the house and returned about an hour later.

"What did the village head say?" I asked.

"I haven't been there."

"So where have you been all this time?"

"On my way into the village I saw Mak Ria in front of the house. I spoke to her. They are family after all."

Mak Ria is Ruben's mother and lives in the house next door. Her youngest brother is married to Wati's younger sister so they are related. That was why Wati wanted to handle the affair as a family matter and not take it straight to the village head. It appeared that Ruben often put pressure on his mother and would not let her tell his father. Father and son did not get on with one another and this was yet another affair that was not to be brought to his father's attention.

I was glad that we had invited the leaders and elders in the church to come and pray for the church that evening. We especially wanted to pray for the young people of the village, that they might get a new perspective for their lives and become open to God. It was the first time we had set up such a prayer evening. That evening the children's and youth leaders and helpers came over, as well as the two elders who had been there the night before to revise the texts and had heard the story about Ruben. Ibu Ann, an Indonesian colleague, had come over from Manna. Some of the young people who were at school in Manna lived in her house. We prayed for the whole of the congregation, each group, all the various leaders and helpers, the elders and then for the young people. We asked God to come into their lives and give them a meaning to their lives that was worth living for. We prayed especially that God would intervene in the tangled situation with Ruben. We had no answers. Around midnight most people went home.

The next morning Ibu Ann was sitting by the front door in my living room, waiting for me to take her back to Manna. I had just popped into the kitchen to get some of the wild boar meat that we got the day before, for her to take home. Wati was behind the house, in the bathroom. Suddenly, we heard a panic-stricken, piercing cry from below our property. What ever had happened? I rushed out of the kitchen into the living room. When I reached the back door, I could see Ruben through the window. He was wearing only shorts and in his hand he was carrying a big machete, a dangerous weapon that the people in the village used as an axe to chop down trees. Slowly I watched as one of Ruben's cousins, who was friendly with him and about his age came running after him. He was talking to him, trying to calm him

161

down, and taking the machete out of his hand. The next moment his older brother joined him and together they led Ruben away.

When Wati came in, we looked at each other, baffled. We couldn't make sense of any of the recent events. Why had Ruben approached us with his machete? What had happened? And why was the whole clan gathered next door at Pak Ria's house?

Ibu Ann went to find out. Slowly it all became clear. The men of the clan had gathered together in the house opposite to discuss wedding preparations for one of the cousins. The scream had come from Ruben's sister, who had realised her brother's intentions when he was leaving the house.

But what had made Ruben so mad?

We discovered that Ruben's inappropriate action towards Wati two days before had spread all through the village and had even reached the house in Manna where his sister was living. When he heard this, Ruben became so enraged that he grabbed the machete, determined to kill Wati, the obvious cause of the gossip, there and then. No wonder his sister had screamed as though it was her own life that was in danger.

The deliberations within the family went on for quite a while. Finally, Pak Ipi, the oldest cousin, said to Ruben, "Either you go up there now and apologise to them, or they are to report you to the police in Manna. It is your choice. I will send them to the police station myself if you don't apologise."

After a moment's hesitation, Ruben went back into the house. A few minutes later he appeared again, wearing trousers and a shirt, and came across to us.

Wati and I invited him to sit down and talk with us about it.

"I am sorry for what happened," he said.

"Why did you do it? What was the reason behind it?"

Slowly, he told us what had made him so mad. We talked about it for quite a while.

At the end he asked us, "Can you forgive me?"

"Yes, we forgive you from the heart. But if people are talking about this all around the area, you have to realise that we were not the ones who spread the gossip."

Then I had a thought. "As a sign of our reconciliation I would like to invite you to a picnic at the beach in Linau. You can choose yourself which of your friends to bring along. Then everyone can see that there is nothing more between us."

Ruben was taken aback, but accepted the invitation gladly. Before he went, we prayed together.

In the afternoon, I popped in to see Pak Ipi. "Pak Ipi, just so you are not left wondering, as a sign of our reconciliation I have invited Ruben and his friends on a picnic to Linau." He was sceptical as to whether that was a good idea. But I reassured him that I was not afraid.

The next day, I was out in the car with Wati. On our way to the market in the next village, we met the two church elders. I stopped to pick them up. Talking about the events of the previous days, one of them said, "Praying didn't help at all. Everything only got a lot worse."

"On the contrary," Wati and I answered together. "That was an answer to our prayer."

Of course we hadn't prayed that Ruben would threaten us with his machete, but that event did lead to dialogue and reconciliation.

It is just that God's ways are not like our ways.

# Chapter 51

# The Toothless Cat

It had been a few weeks since the young people had brought us any wild boar meat, and Wati and I were wondering what we should cook. We talked about delicious dishes, which we had no means of preparing, and made each other hungry.

"The best *bakso*[32] I have ever eaten I had in Jakarta, at a Chinese restaurant," Wati said. "They told me the cook made it out of cat meat. It was absolutely delicious."

That afternoon we were invited to a prayer meeting at Mak Warin's. On our way, we met a few men from our church who were repairing the path to the church.

"Where are you off to?" they asked.

"To the prayer meeting at Mak Warin's. Why don't you come and join us?" we invited them, but none of them responded.

Mak Warin's house was nearby, just across the road that went through our village. It was the first house on the large village square. While we were waiting for others to arrive, we asked about family news.

"How is Warin? Is he still up in the mountains?"

"Yes, I am planning to go and visit him next month," his mother told us.

Warin was her oldest son. He was clearing a piece of forest for himself in order to plant coffee. There was simply not enough land in the village for the many young people there. Whilst we were chatting, her cat came running over. It was holding its head to one side and seemed to be generally disturbed. There was a nick on its ear.

"Is this your cat?" I asked.

"Yes."

"Where did it get this nick on its ear from? Did it get it in a fight with another cat?"

"No, I did that myself with a knife."

"Why would you do that?" I asked in surprise.

"To help me recognise it."

"Poor cat. It seems so lopsided that it can't see straight."

---

[32] *Bakso* are small meatballs in broth.

164

"It's not that bad," she replied. "The worst thing is that it doesn't seem to be catching any rats. It's afraid of them."

"How is that possible?"

"Well, it doesn't have any teeth so it runs away when it sees a rat. They are really taking over as they are not afraid of the cat!"

We would not have believed it if we hadn't seen it with our own eyes. The poor cat! It was missing out on its purpose in life because it had no teeth and was not able to catch rats. Then I had an idea.

"If you give me your toothless cat, I will give you a kitten with teeth. But only if you don't make a cut in its ear."

"Yes, all right. You can have it. But what are you going to do with it?"

I hesitated. "Wati tells me that cat meat is rather tasty. During the war people ate cats in Germany as well. They called them roof rabbits."

It was her turn to be surprised.

"You really want to eat the cat?"

I looked at Wati and winked. "Why not? We could at least try it."

"How will you take it so that it doesn't run away from you?"

"If you put a cat in a sack or a pillow case it can't fight back and you can carry it without any problem."

With that our deal was done.

"Do you want to take the cat straight away?"

I assumed the men would still be working in front of the church and would ask silly questions, so I said, "No. Noel[33] can bring it over and pick up the kitten at the same time. We will go home first."

Just as well – the men really were still hard at work, but we had only been home about five minutes when Noel arrived with the cat in a pillow case.

"Did anyone say anything to you on the way?" I asked.

"Yes, the men working in front of the church asked where I was going and I told them I was going to see you."

"Did they notice what you were carrying?" I wanted to know.

"I didn't tell them. But then the cat mewed and they wanted to know what I was doing with a cat in my sack. So I told them."

So the cat was out of the bag after all. There was nothing we could do to change that! Wati prepared the cat and we both enjoyed it. And that remained village gossip for a long time!

---

[33] Noel is her younger son.

# Chapter 52

# Lost – Christmas in the Mountains

"Could you pick us up at four o'clock at Talang Sebaris?" I asked Turen, who owned a four-wheel drive, apparently of German build from the year 1951, so about 40 years old!

"Us" – that was me as driver, Wati, Sida, two Bible school students and a few of the young people, 12 of us in all. We had left Napal Melintang in the morning and were on our way to Padang Capau, right up in the mountains, to celebrate Christmas with a few of the young families from our village who had settled there. They were clearing areas of forest in the mountains in order to plant coffee and to establish a new life for themselves.

How fortuitous to bump into Turen around midday at the turning at Suka Raja, where the extensive rubber plantation, set up by the government, began. He agreed, so saving us a good ten kilometres hike into the mountains. It had rained a lot during the previous weeks, and so the road was impassable for my car. Now we had enough time to visit a few Christians on the rubber plantation and to invite them to a Christmas service the following evening.

Turen even arrived on time at the agreed place. He knew the way and was aware that there was always the chance that unpredictable things could happen. Although it should take no more than two hours for us to reach our destination, he didn't want to be caught out by darkness on this road.

Wati and I sat down on the passenger seat next to the driver. It was only a wooden plank. The car had no roof, just a frame, and there were no seats in the back to sit on. The young people climbed into the back and held on to the frame, glad not to have to walk. We prayed before we set off on an adventurous journey.

The road up to the small market area at Talang Tebat, at the end of the rubber plantation, seemed like one big mud hole. The mud wasn't deep and as there was gravel underneath it, the car managed beautifully.

Turen decided to take a short break. He put chains around the tyres and bought a small bottle of brake fluid. In answer to my question, he explained that his brake hose was leaking. A shiver ran through me but I comforted myself with the thought that you could not drive fast along those roads anyway. A good driver, if he is astute, would drive downhill in low gear and avoid braking as much as possible. I still remembered the road from my previous visits. We had no real trouble making the first long, steep incline. Turen stopped, walked round the car, and asked me to get out. It was then that I realized that I was sitting on a box. He opened it, got out a water canister and poured the water into the cooler, making it steam. He repeated this performance after every incline, and filled up the canister at the next spring we came across. We used up eight canisters of water on that journey. I was so thankful that at least the engine, the wheels and the steering, which I figure are of the utmost importance when driving, seemed to be in order.

Then we came across the first big mud hole. It was probably over 50 metres long. Turen drove into it at an angle so as not to get stuck. We all had to hold on tight in order not to fall over board. The engine roared as we crawled slowly forward. He had a bit of trouble driving out, but managed it at the second attempt. At the next mud hole, we all decided to get out and walk round it on foot. It was dusk when we finally arrived in Padang Capau. We all agreed that we'd much rather walk back than get a lift with this car.

The next morning at nine o'clock, the Christmas service was held in the small meeting hut which the Christians had built next to the main path. Because of this, the settlement had already started to be called Talang Gereja (Church spot). Some of the Christians from the vicinity also came to the service. Pastor Rusdi, who was the speaker for the day, had come up the day before from Bengkulu. After the service we visited all the Christian families. In each house we sang Christmas songs, prayed for the family, were offered refreshments, and then moved on to the next house, the way we did in our own village. Here, though, the houses were often far apart. The way to one house was over a deep ravine. A thick tree trunk had been laid across the ravine and I was scared when I realised we would have to cross it to reach the house.

"There's no way I am going across that," I declared. "I'll wait here until you come back."

"But we are not coming back the same way," Pastor Rusdi explained. "You have to come."

"I can't!" I protested. "I feel sick just looking into the ravine."

"I'll lead you across," Pak Rusdi suggested.

Finally, I grabbed his hand and trusted myself to his leading. I kept looking straight ahead while he led me across the tree trunk as though I were a blind person.

We still had a 20 minute climb up the mountain to visit the last family. On the way we were surprised by a rain shower and all of us got soaked. However, we had a real dinner at the family's home. When we began our way back, refreshed and strengthened, it was still overcast but at least it was not raining.

Pastor Rusdi offered to take my bag on his motorbike. I gladly accepted his offer and gave him the bag with my overnight things. The red muddy earth was soft and slippery from the rain. A thick layer of red mud soon stuck to the soles of our flip flops and, because it was much easier to walk barefoot I took them off, like the others, and carried them in my hands until someone offered to carry them for me. Barefoot, our trek back took us up and down, up and down through the mountains.

A few Christians lived along the way. Pak Rusdi was waiting for us at one of the houses where we sang and prayed with the family who invited us to eat rice with them. Other Christians stopped us along the road and invited us into their huts. In that way we were able to pass on something of the Christmas joy over and over again. Some of our group had gone on ahead, and I was with three or four others who brought up the rear.

It was already passed four o'clock when we finally arrived in the village of Talang Tebat. I thought that those of our group who had gone ahead would be waiting for us there, but they had already gone on. I could not even see Turen and his car. Pity. My feet were sore, and I would have quite liked a ride for the last few kilometres, but there were no other cars there. We could not afford to take a long rest as there was a Christmas service that evening at Talang Sebaris where I had left my car the day before, and we did not want to be late for the service.

The path became now even trickier to walk on. At one time the road had been filled with gravel and the sharp stones cut into the softened soles of my feet. My flip flops had gone on with the group ahead of us. Slowly, I dragged myself on.

"How far is it to the turning to Talang Sebaris?" we asked some passersby.

"It's just about two kilometres," they told us, "but you could take a short cut. You would save almost half an hour. It goes into the forest further down there. We are going that way too."

"And what is this path like?" I asked anxiously.

"It's a narrow path, but only wet in one place."

We decided to take the short cut as by now it was almost six o'clock, and it would soon be dark.

"Well," I thought, "It's just as well that the others will already be there."

I found that path much easier to walk on because there were no stones. Again a group of men passed us, walking quickly. We greeted them.

"This is no place to bring tourists," they told those who were with me. They could see I was exhausted. I was, but we simply laughed at their suggestion. It was almost dark when we finally arrived at the home of the Ri-man family in Talang Sebaris.

Having greeted us, they asked, "Where are the others?"

"They should have arrived here ages ago."

"But they aren't here yet."

"That's not possible. They were ahead of us and we stopped several times."

"We've not seen them yet."

"What about Pak Rusdi?" I asked. "Has he arrived?"

"He has already gone over to the service. It is starting in ten minutes."

"We still have to wash. We can't go to the service like this. Where did Pak Rusdi leave my bag?"

"Your bag is here in the bedroom. There is a water hole behind the house where you can wash."

The cool water felt good and I was so glad to be able to put on fresh clothes. I didn't have any shoes though, so I went to the service barefoot. It had already started and we squeezed ourselves quietly into a row of free chairs. We had barely sat down when the singing group from Napal Melin-tang was called up to sing. I gave the preacher, who was leading the service, a signal to say that we were not ready. After all, the group hadn't arrived but he didn't know that. He thought that because I was there, the group was also there.

"What should we sing if we are called up again?" I asked Wati.

"How about 'Angels from the realms of glory'," she suggested. "That's in the hymn book." The guitarist from Bengkulu was sitting in front of us. "Would you accompany us on your guitar?" I whispered in his ear. He agreed. The singing group from Napal Melintang was announced once again. We stood up and sang the song, without having practised it. I stood at the back of the group so no-one could see that I was barefooted. Later, we sang a second song.

Immediately after the service, Pak Rusdi came up to us. "Where are the others?" he asked.

"We don't know. We haven't seen anyone else. We took the short cut."

"Perhaps, they've got lost," someone suggested. "Perhaps, they didn't know where the turning was and carried on walking straight ahead."

"And where does that go?"

"Straight through the rubber plantation. You have to walk almost two hours before you get to the next village," the local people told us.

"Surely, they would have realised quite quickly that they were going wrong and would have turned back."

"Maybe, but they are still not here."

The discussions went on a little while longer about where and how they might have got lost. Everyone was agreed – we needed to search for them. The men were seriously worried about the young people. They got some lanterns and set off.

I was less concerned. After all, it was a group of about seven people, not only girls, and a few of them were already over 20. The two Bible school students were also with them. I expected that they would have found shelter somewhere and had decided to stay there for the night. After the strain of the day, I was really too tired to be too worried so I committed them into God's care and slept like a log. It was already light when I woke up the next morning.

"Have the young people turned up yet?" I asked as soon as I saw the preacher.

"No, and the men are not back either. I am about to go and search for them myself."

After breakfast, I drove to Suka Raja with those of the group who were with me, to make a few more visits. There we met a totally exhausted Pak Rusdi. He had spent the whole night searching along with two search parties. It appeared that they had heard calls for help, but could find no-one.

"Why don't I drive to the village they would have arrived at had they stayed on the road?" I suggested. "How do I find it?"

"You would have to drive the long way round. It is about 20 kilometres, so it's about an hour's drive."

I drove off and found the village.

"Do you know if seven young people turned up here last night?" I asked at one of the first houses.

"Yes, they were here. They asked us to take them across to Talang Sebaris last night. But we couldn't and wouldn't let them go alone so they stayed overnight at the house of the village head. They set off this morning."

Relieved, we thanked them and drove back to let Pak Rusdi know.

It was after midday before we were all finally reunited.

"Didn't you realise that you had gone the wrong way?" I asked one of them.

"Yes, we did, quite early on."

"So why didn't you turn back?"

"Well, we figured we'd carry on walking until we met someone to ask the way."

"Well?"

"We didn't come across anyone."

# Chapter 53

# Crossing to Pontianak

"What do we do now?" I looked at Sida, at a complete loss as to what we should do.

Exhausted, we were both sitting with our luggage in front of the PELNI building in Jakarta, the Indonesian company for boat passengers. It was almost midday and we were both hungry.

We had arrived in Jakarta that morning after a 15-hour journey on the night bus from Malang, East Java. We had attended the yearly faith conference of the Indonesian Missionary Fellowship in Batu, East Java, and now we wanted to continue on to Western Kalimantan. Sida wanted to go to Bible school, in Nanga Lebang, not far from Sintang, in the heart of Kalimantan. It was the only Bible School that would accept her as she had not completed High School. She had a comprehensive Bible knowledge however, having worked for years with the children at church and with me on the Bible translation.

After our arrival in Jakarta that morning we had gone straight to the airport. There were no more tickets on sale there and we were sent into town to the travel agency. There we were informed that all flights to Pontianak, Western Kalimantan, were fully booked for the next ten days because of the holidays. That was too late for the start of Sida's course. My last hope was the PELNI boat, which was due to leave the following day. We spent an hour in a taxi driving through the megacity that is Jakarta, but there, too, everything was fully booked. Even my white skin did not help me get a tourist ticket. It all seemed quite hopeless.

We prayed together and asked God for a solution.

A man approached us and asked, "Do you really want to go to Pontianak?"

Surprised, we said we did.

"I know of a cargo ship that sails tonight. They could take you. If you like, I'll take you there."

We looked at each other, feeling somewhat incredulous. Should we trust this man? Was he possibly even the answer to our prayers?

Actually, we really did not have a choice as we had tried everything else. So we went with the stranger who took us to a small house near the port. A lady sold us two tickets to Pontianak. They cost as much as the cheapest PELNI tickets.

"The boat leaves tonight," the man who had helped us explained. "I will take you to the boat on my motorbike this afternoon at 3 o'clock."

That meant we had a couple of hours spare, time enough to find something to eat. We returned at the agreed time.

The man greeted us. "First of all, I'll take Sida with her luggage to the boat. Then I'll come back and get you."

A quarter of an hour later he was back. I sat side-saddle on the back of the motorbike. "We'll just do a little detour to avoid the control post," he said. "If anyone asks, we'll say that I am showing you round the port."

It appeared, then, that it was not all above board. It was probably best not to ask any more questions. We drove around the port a little and then he steered towards a ship. It was a handsome old wooden barge. We walked up the gang plank.

We had to climb over people who had made themselves comfortable in the gangways. Then we bumped into the captain. "Who is this woman?" he asked my escort.

"She is German, a passenger," he replied.

"Sorry. Not possible," he explained. "We are not allowed to take foreigners unless we have the express permission of the port authorities."

"And where can we get this permission?" I demanded.

"Go to the port authorities and ask them issue the permit. Then you can come back."

I doubted that we would be able to manage that in time before the ship sailed.

The man took me to the port authorities, which was only two blocks away, and waited outside. I was warmly welcomed.

"I need a permit to be able to travel on the freight ship to Pontianak. Would you be able to issue one?"

"No, unfortunately we can't. Only the central office can do that."

"And where is the central office?" I inquired.

"It's in the city centre, but they will be closed by now. You'll have to go tomorrow morning."

"And you really can't issue the permit yourself?" I wasn't going to let it go.

"No, we don't have the right form."

"What is the issue?"

"You have to sign that you will not make a claim if the ship sinks and you are injured or even die. You have to go into the city to do that."

I gave up.

Outside I explained to the man that I had to get the permit in the city. He took me back to the house where we had bought the tickets. Then he collected Sida and our luggage from the ship. I was disappointed that we were not able to set off for Pontianak that day after all. On the other hand, I also felt a sense of relief that in that way the authorities were at least aware of my whereabouts. In those waters, it does happen from time to time that a boat sinks.

It was already getting dark when Sida arrived. She was very relieved to see me.

"There is another boat tomorrow," the man told us. "You could go on that."

"Fine. Where can we stay overnight?"

"You can sleep in the corridor on the first floor," the lady who had sold us the tickets offered. "There are a few pillows. You may use those."

"And where is the bathroom?"

"We don't have enough water for a shower, and the toilet is blocked. You'll need to go to a public toilet." What a great prospect!

Still, we decided to stay there for the night. We were too tired and exhausted to spend ages looking for alternative overnight accommodation. So we settled down to sleep on the bare planked floor and covered ourselves with our *kain*. We were the only overnight guests.

The next morning the sun woke us before six o'clock. We stretched our stiff limbs. I was glad to get up off the hard floor. The first thing we did was to take time to read quietly from the Bible and to pray. After a while Sida came out with, "Ibu, where do you think north is?"

Mystified, I thought for a moment. "North? I guess it's that way." I pointed with my finger. "That's the direction of the sea, the direction of Pontianak. Why do you ask?"

"Well, it says here in my Bible, 'You have made your way around here long enough; now turn north' (Deut. 2:3)."

"That's appropriate," I said, encouraging her.

I too had read an encouraging Bible passage. When the king had offered Ezra soldiers to protect and accompany him on the long journey to Jerusalem, he had refused the offer, the reason being that God would be his protection. God's promise was enough. That gave me confidence regarding my own journey. He would protect me.

We spent the morning in the city. The port authority was not hard to find. After I had signed that in the case of injury or death I would forfeit any claim, they issued me with the permit to cross on the cargo ship. We still

173

had time and so we drove to the Monas, the Indonesian national monument in the centre of Jakarta, a symbol of independence. Inside we visited the museum of the War of Independence from Dutch colonial rule.

In the afternoon, we were once again taken to the boat in turn. This time it was not a wooden barge, but a smaller metal ship. Sida and I were just working out where we should set up our base for the next few days – we did not even have a mat we could spread out – when a sailor came up to us. He introduced himself as the first mate.

"Where are you going?"

"To Sintang."

"I see you have a guitar. Great!"

"It is Sida's. She is going to Bible school in Kalimantan."

"Are you Christians?" he asked happily. "I am a Christian too. The captain is as well. He is an Adventist. But he is not coming on board until this evening."

We were all happy to have found siblings in the faith.

"Where will you sleep at night?" he asked us.

"We are not sure yet."

"Would you like a cabin?"

"If that is possible then, yes, please. I thought this was a cargo ship and that there weren't any cabins for passengers."

"That's true, but the sailors often rent out their cabins to passengers."

Sida went with him to have a look while I stayed with the luggage.

When she got back, I said, "Right, let's take our luggage to the cabin," but Sida seemed somewhat bothered.

"Ibu, I don't know. The room is so tiny. Why don't you go and have a look for yourself?"

"Sida, I don't think we have any other choice. Where will we spend the night otherwise? Cabins are small. If that is all it is, then let's take it." I paid for the cabin and we set off with our luggage.

Below deck the gangways were buzzing with passengers. I discovered a sign: "Kamar mandi". Bathroom. It's always good to know where the facilities are. Then Sida led me through a door into what seemed to be the boat's kitchen. There were a few cookers in the room and steam was coming out of big pots. In the room behind there were two large tables with benches. There were people there, too. Then she opened a side door and we were in a cabin. At the most it measured 1 x 2 metres. The lower bunk was already occupied by a grandmother and her granddaughter, as well as their luggage. The top bunk was still free for us. It was no more than 75cm wide. About a metre above it was a hatch that opened. Now I understood what Sida had meant.

"How are we both supposed to sleep here?" Sida asked me, dubiously.

"Hmm, probably one after the other," I suggested.

But it was too early to sleep so we went back on deck and watched the to-ing and fro-ing. The cargo, which consisted of many sacks of potatoes, was still being loaded.

The first mate approached us. "The captain has arrived. He would like to meet you."

We followed him onto the bridge. The captain greeted us cheerfully and asked what we were doing, where we were from and where we were going. We readily answered his questions. He himself was from Manado. He was small and round and I guessed he was in his mid-forties.

"When will we set sail?" I asked before we took our leave.

"In the early hours."

"There is a bit of time to go then."

"Yes, but everyone has to be on board tonight so that we can leave as soon as all the cargo is loaded."

As we left, he invited us to visit him on the bridge at any time. I decided to make the most of his invitation as there was an excellent view from the bridge.

It was late. Sida and I were both very tired and wanted to rest. Sida agreed that I should go to bed first. In the room in front of the cabin there was still a lot of commotion. The air in the cabin was sticky and hot but I was so tired that I fell fast asleep anyway.

Suddenly, I was roughly wakened. "Ibu, when can I sleep?" I heard Sida's plaintive voice.

"What's the time?"

"It's already almost four."

"Oh, I am so sorry. Where have you been all night?"

"I waited outside in front of the cabin."

"I am so sorry. I am glad you woke me up."

I got up and left the bed to her. After I had freshened up a bit, I climbed on deck. The cool morning air hit me and it felt great. It was still dark. The workers were still busy loading up cargo and it was long after daylight before we finally set sail. Out at sea the engines were switched on. I decided to go and visit the captain. He was happy to see me and invited me in.

"Have you eaten?" he asked me.

"No," I answered truthfully.

Immediately, he ordered a portion of *Supermie*[34] for each of us from the ship's kitchen.

I looked around the bridge. There were a series of technical instruments I did not understand. The captain told me that he had collected the ship from Japan a few months before. "It was a few years old, but it still had all the original Japanese instruments," he explained. I felt reassured. "It even had a radar system and could automatically steer around obstacles." That too was reassuring, considering that in those waters there were numerous coral reefs. He explained a few more of the instruments to me. I watched how he determined our position and entered it into the log.

When the noodles were brought, he apologised that he was not able to offer me a set table. The noodles were steaming and still far too hot to eat. After the meal, he told me that he had only been a Christian for a few years. A conversation about faith followed.

Sida was awake when I returned to the cabin and was not feeling at all well. By then we were on the high seas and the ship was swaying. She ate nothing for the two days we were at sea. Most of the other passengers were the same. I kept going to see the captain on the bridge and as the ship seemed to sway the least up there, I did not feel too bad.

The following night, Sida kept being sick and I could hardly chase her off the bunk. In the end we agreed that we would sleep at either end of the bed. We stretched our feet towards one other, something which is actually considered offensive in Sida's culture, and slept half sitting up. We got a little fresh air through the hatch in the ceiling even though we also kept getting a whiff of the exhaust fumes from the chimney.

Suddenly, the door opened.

"Good morning. Would you like some potatoes for breakfast?" A laughing first mate appeared at the door and held a bowl full of steaming new potatoes under my nose.

When he noticed my hesitation, he added, "Take it. It's fine," and put the bowl on my lap. I just about managed a whispered, "Terima kasih, thank you", before he closed the door again.

It was only half past five but I was fully awake. Sida was still not feeling well and was not interested in the potatoes. Our cabin cohabitants also declined. I ate a few of the potatoes and felt strengthened for a second day on the boat. Most of that day, I spent either reading my book or with the captain on the bridge. He appeared to feel honoured by my visits. The weather

---

[34] *Supermie* is the Indonesia version of Supernoodles, a popular Indonesian ready dish.

stayed calm. Sun and cloud interchanged and the wind stayed gentle. Still, most passengers were fighting sea sickness and moved very little. I estimated that there were more than a hundred passengers below deck. In order for them to get enough fresh air, a hatch had been left slightly open which, I thought, probably did not conform to safety regulations.

When I woke up the next morning, I noticed immediately that the engines were quieter. I went on deck. It was already daylight, and we were no longer on the open sea. Trees lined the shore on either side of the ship. I went up to see the captain on the bridge.

"Where are we?" I asked, interested.

"We are now at the delta of the Kapuas[35]," the captain explained. "In about an hour we will stop briefly at a landing platform. Most of the passengers will leave us then. You can continue until we get to the port. That's another half an hour or so further on." I took Sida the good news that we were nearly there.

Back on dry land, we are truly thankful to have firm ground beneath our feet again even though we still had the impression that the ground was moving.

---

[35] The *Kapuas* is the big river in western Kalimantan, on which Pontianak lies.

# Chapter 54

# In Nanga Lebang

Sida and I travelled by bus to Sintang, a district town of Western Kalimantan, and then got in a motor boat to take us up the Kapuas. The Kapuas is a wide river which ambles gently along. The boat, an open barge with an awning and full of wooden seats, was already quite full. At the landing platform, the passengers pushed and shoved to get on board with their luggage. These were people from the villages upriver who had come down to the district town to do their errands. The journey to the Bible School in Nanga Lebang would take about four hours.

Sida and I did not chat much. Both of us were deep in thought. Sida was about to begin a new chapter in her life. She was in her late twenties and was once again about to start studying. She had expressed the wish to go to Bible school so that she would be able to get more deeply involved in our congregation as a proper member of staff. Our journey to Sintang had been full of adventure but God had encouraged us while we were in Jakarta through a definite word for our situation. He was going ahead of us, and we knew we could trust him.

There was a lot of traffic on the river in Sintang, but after about half an hour's ride, it became much quieter. There was a peculiar calm around. The only sounds we could hear were the regular humming of the engine and the occasional cry of an animal from the jungle which lined the river on either side. The river banks rose up about two to three metres. Further up in the trees, I could see a clear line demarcated by dried reeds. Below that, the leaves were caked with mud, a clear indication that the water had not too long ago risen all the way up there. Later, I heard that the water level in the dry season could easily drop a further five metres. The less water there is in the river, the stronger and more dangerous its current. I noticed that there were no palm trees or any other indication of villages along the banks, except once in a while a small vegetable plot on the banks where the mud, deposited by the flooding, had rendered the soil fertile. Only rarely did I see a landing platform. Moreover, we only stopped once or twice before we reached our destination. I had the impression that we were travelling through thick jungle where no-one was living for miles around.

Finally, we stopped at the wide landing platform at Nanga Lebang, our destination. A young man greeted us and led us up the long wooden pier, which was at least 100 metres long, before we stepped on to dry land. We crossed a big meadow and there, on the other side, under gigantic trees were various wooden barracks, built on stilts about one metre high. This was the Bible school and included the living quarters of both staff and students. As there were still three days before the start of the new academic year, Sida and I were put up with the Australian missionary couple Bruce and Annette, who had founded the Bible school many years earlier. They even had water in the house, so we did not have to go down to the river to bathe.

Bruce showed us around the grounds, the class rooms and the quarters for the students. On our way round, we met the Indonesian principal and a few of the Indonesian teachers. Bruce showed us his office, where he had a small radio transceiver. He had used it to keep in daily contact with his co-workers who were scattered around the jungle but at that time he rarely used the apparatus.

The next day, Sida and I explored the surroundings on our own. We wanted to visit the small local church. A track led through the forest and over a narrow bridge across a stream. Soon, we were above the Kapuas and next to the small church. As so many people came to the services by boat, it had its own landing platform at the river. Not far away were a few shops. They were really house boats with wide platforms, anchored to the bank with ropes. Thick, narrow planks connected them to the bank and to each other. Sida wanted to buy a few things and so we dared to go across these wobbly bridges with no railings to hold on to. In the afternoon, we walked around the Bible school grounds again. Sida wondered, "Ibu, what kind of terrain do you think this is?" She was shaking her head. I couldn't understand what she wanted to say.

"What do you mean?"

"Well, Ibu, haven't you noticed? There are lots of trees and everything is green, but there are no flowers and no fruit trees."

"Oh, you mean these trees. Are they not fruit trees?"

"No, these are all jungle trees."

I had not noticed that, and only then realised that I had not seen any banana plants or coconut palms.

She continued, "There are also no cars or roads. There is just a landing strip."

"Where did you see that?" I ask.

"Well, that meadow down by the river, which we crossed when we arrived. That is a landing strip." That had never occurred to me.

Later, Bruce explained that the soil in the area was so poor that no fruit trees would grow there.

On our walk the next day, Sida stopped suddenly. "Ibu," she asked, "could you bear working here?"

I had to think for a moment. I wanted to answer her truthfully. It was a remote area, much lonelier and simpler than our village of Napal Melintang in Sumatra. I realised she had not imagined what it would be like. For me, such outward things were not so important, but I was not sure that I would want to voluntarily work there either.

So I replied, "If God had called me here, then I could imagine working here."

Sida looked at me thoughtfully for a moment and then her decision was made.

"Then I can too," she answered resolutely.

# Chapter 55

# It is not Good to Distress Your Guests

It was early afternoon. Two of the young people were walking quickly up the path to my house in the village of Napal Melintang. I went to the front door and opened it.

"Two Westerners have arrived, a man and a lady," they reported, still slightly out of breath. "They want to visit you."

"That's curious," I thought. "I'm not expecting any foreign guests."

I followed the two young people down to the road. Indeed, there were two white people: a lady, about my age, and an older gentleman. It was Dagmar Becker, a former class mate, and her father.

"What a surprise! Welcome!" I greeted them.

They were visibly relieved to have found me and went with me up to my house. While Yal, one of the students from the village who helped me in the house during her summer holidays, brought us refreshments, the two told me their story.

"We have been to Indonesia several times and have visited Bali, Sulawesi and other parts of the country. Now we thought we would come and visit you."

"That is lovely but how on earth did you find me?" I wanted to know.

"We asked your parents for your address."

"But that is just a post office box address in Manna."

"Well, when we got to Bengkulu this morning, we showed the taxi driver your address. He told us that he knew you and where the village was. But then he still had to ask around several times."

I smiled. "I expect he didn't want to lose your business. Still, he managed to find me."

We were still chatting when a neighbour arrived.

"My sister-in-law's baby is seriously ill. Could you come and have a look?" she asked me.

I excused myself and promised my visitors I would not be long.

The baby really was seriously ill and I didn't know what to do.

"We should take it to the doctor's."

There was a state-run health clinic in the neighbouring village, where a Christian doctor, with whom we had a good relationship, had recently started working. That was where I had taken the mother to give birth in the first place. The family agreed and I went back home to get the car keys.

"The baby is really ill. I am going to take it to the doctor in next village," I explained to my guests. "I should be back in about an hour. You are welcome to make yourselves comfortable in your room. Yal will show you."

The family was already waiting by the time I had got the car out of the garage. A few more young people climbed on the seats in the cargo area. "Oh well," I thought, "I'm only going three kilometres and it's not putting anyone out."

About 100 metres before we reached the health clinic, I noticed that something wasn't right with the car. I got out and looked at the wheels. We had a flat tyre. The family walked the remaining 100 metres to the clinic. I was glad the young people were there and could help me change the tyre. Although they had never done such a thing before, they threw themselves into the task with great enthusiasm and, following my instructions, managed well. Once the tyre had been successfully changed, I followed the family to the clinic. By then the doctor had examined the baby, but because it had such a high temperature and as he was not a paediatrician, he advised us to take the baby to the hospital in Manna.

The family agreed and we drove the twenty kilometres to the hospital. I left the family at the hospital and drove on to get my tyre mended. When I returned, I was told that the baby had been admitted and the mother was staying with it. The rest of the family returned to the village with me. Several hours had passed, and dusk was falling by the time I got home. My guests were sitting on the little bench in front of the house, waiting for me.

The next day, I drove them to Manna to register them with the police. The policemen at the police station were always happy when I arrived with my guests. It brought a little change into their rather dull, daily routine, and made them feel very important. The policeman, himself, filled in the necessary forms and although he had the passports in front of him, kept asking questions.

"Surname?"

"Becker."

"Oh, Boris Becker," another commented.

"Yes, that is my son," Mr. Becker said. I translated and everyone laughed. The joke worked and the ice was broken. It took almost an hour to fill in the two forms and we could leave the police station.

"I have to go to Manna again today," I told my guests the following day. "I have a meeting at four o'clock with some church representatives there. I hope to be home in time for the evening meal. If you need anything, then ask Yal."

With those words I left my guests in the care of the student, who understood no English apart from "Good morning" and "Thank you".

After doing a bit of shopping, I arrived on time at the designated place with the hope that we would soon be able to start. The host opened the door and gave me a bewildered look. I felt confused too.

"The meeting is today, isn't it?" I asked after we had greeted one another.

"Yes, of course. Come in!"

I sat down in the living room. None of the others were there. The lady of the house greeted me and brought me a drink. Then she excused herself as she had things to do in the kitchen. The man sat down next to me and we started an awkward conversation. The meeting had originally been organised for the evening, but I had insisted on the afternoon because I wanted to get back to the village before dark.

I thought about my guests waiting at home and looked surreptitiously at the clock. It was after five o'clock before another participant arrived. We continued talking. Then I tried again.

"Would we be able to start please? I have to leave in an hour at the latest," I said, pressing my concern.

"But the food isn't ready yet," the host protested. "We'll start the meeting with a meal."

"Oh dear," I thought, then suggested, "Couldn't we just start, and when the food is ready, take a break? I really do have to leave in an hour as I have guests at home." I knew that even if I left during the break, it would still be after seven o'clock and pitch dark by the time I reached home.

Finally, I got my way and we started the discussion when the last of the participants arrived. We hadn't got very far before the food was ready. I prepared to leave as it was already getting dark outside.

"Why are you leaving already?" the host protested.

"But I told you that I have guests at home who are waiting for me."

"But that is no reason to go."

"Yes, it is. They are guests from back home in Germany." That seemed to have made an impression, but he was still not convinced that I had to leave.

"I have to give them their dinner and look after them," I added, trying to explain how I felt.

"Didn't you leave them anything to eat?"

"Yes, of course. But they won't start eating without me."

"But why not? They can eat if they are hungry."

"But they won't."

Still no-one seemed to understand. The discussion revolved around why my guests were not able to help themselves. Surely, any normal person would do that if they were hungry.

"They won't help themselves while I am not there," I explained, "because in Germany it is not customary for guests to eat without their host." They still looked at me, obviously not really understanding.

Finally, the hostess pitched in. "Well, if that is the case," she said, "then you must go home. It's not good to distress your guests." I marvelled at her perception and wisdom. "But," she continued, "before you go, you must eat something." Everyone agreed with that.

When I reached home and walked through the gate, I could see my guests, sitting in the dark on the little bench and looking at the stars. Even though Yal had put their meal in front of them and had signalled to them to help themselves, they had not started to eat.

"We wanted to wait for you," they said.

# Chapter 56

# Church Split

The next day was Christmas Eve. The Christmas service, hosted by our congregation in the village, had taken place two days earlier and had, as always, involved a programme filling the whole evening. As it was a public event, a few policemen from Manna had come and kept watch, in case of trouble. The village head had come in with a great deal of show during the sermon and had left, equally ostentatiously, after his speech. The following day, the way we always did at Christmas, we had visited all the homes of the members of our congregation and prayed for them. For myself, I was in the middle of sorting and packing – in a few days I would be leaving the village forever.

Ten years had passed since I had first celebrated Christmas there in Napal Melintang. At that time, it had all been so new and strange for me. About a year and a half later, I had moved into the village to learn the language of the Serawai people and to translate the New Testament into their mother tongue. I had enjoyed the work. I had liked living there and had grown to love the people. It is true, it had not always been easy and there had been a few times when I had almost had to leave the village.

When Renate was no longer able to extend her visa and had to finish her work at the clinic, the leadership of the mission had strongly suggested that I move to Bengkulu to continue my work from there. I was able to counter that successfully since I would not have left the village if Renate had only gone on home leave to Germany. Anyway, my trained and faithful assistant Sida was in the village and would hardly have moved to Bengkulu with me. And so I was given permission to stay. Later Wati, the nurse, came to continue the clinic. The swimming accident and the slightly obscure threats by the village youth were some of the critical situations we had faced. But each time God had intervened and turned the situation to good.

By then, the translation of the New Testament had been completed, revised and checked and was ready to be handed over to the Bible Society to be printed. Our mission's staff conference would be taking place over New Year in East Java, and after that I planned to go to the Indonesian Bible Society in Bogor, near Jakarta, to discuss some final details with regard to the printing of the New Testament. Following that, I was going on a much-deserved home leave, planning to be home for my mother's seventieth birthday at the end of January. Whether I would return to Indonesia after that or start a new assignment in a different country was still open to question.

Tensions were running high in the village. A few years earlier, the whole of our congregation, as well as most of the other Serawai congregations, had broken away from *GEKISIA*[36] and joined another church union, one associated with the *IMF*[37] , with whom I was working. On a leadership level, this had led to a dispute and to separation. It was all about church politics and had meant little to the members of our congregation. I, too, had preferred to keep out of the dispute as I had wanted to concentrate on the completion of the translation of the New Testament.

Much more recently, some men had arrived in our congregation and had tried, rather unscrupulously, to manipulate our members. These men had left the village without having achieved anything, but below the surface, things had continued to simmer. Different groups and factions had formed as questions were fiercely discussed. I, personally, was on the outside of it all and only picked up a little of what was going on. And yet the villagers sensed that I was not impressed by a church splitting through unclear motives.

The village head, Pak Wil, decided to invite people to his own Christmas service. That had never happened before as we had always celebrated Christmas together. Neither had it ever happened before that the church staff, the preacher, as well as myself, had not been invited to a service at someone's house. Instead, Pak Wil had invited a preacher from the outside. It all seemed a little clandestine and odd.

That morning I wanted to de-register with the police in Manna and say goodbye to a few people I knew in the town. I had already picked up my handbag with my car papers, when Wati came up from the village with the news that the previous evening some people from the village had signed up for membership with the other church. They had been promised education grants for their children, which presumably would turn out to be empty promises, and some had softened in response. I felt very sad.

I went down to the village and drove the car out of the garage. When I closed the garage door, Pak Jaliaman, one of the outside visitors, came

---

[36] *GEKISIA* stands for *Gereja Kristen Injili Se-Indonesia*. As the church *GEKISUS*, the union of *Evangelical Churches of Southern Sumatra* (see introduction), expanded to Jakarta and other parts of Indonesia, it changed its name to *GEKISIA*.

[37] *IMF* is the *Indonesian Missionary Fellowship* to whom I was seconded.

across the village square towards me. He, like myself, belonged to the IMF and we had known each other for years.

We greeted each other rather coolly. He seemed nervous.

"Where are you going?" he asked.

"I have errands to do in Manna."

"I want to talk with you."

In the ensuing conversation back at my house, it appeared that he had not been able to follow what people were discussing the previous night as the villagers had been talking in their local language. He was horrified when he discovered from us the kind of promises that had been made to people to entice them to change their allegiance and he wanted to put it right.

As I walked down the path from my house into the village for a second time, everywhere I could see families sitting together on the porches of their houses. I sensed that the events of the previous evening were their topic of conversation. As I came resolutely down the path, my handbag over my shoulder, the conversations stopped. The people looked at me expectantly.

"Where are you off to?" someone called out.

"To Manna, to the police station," I answered truthfully. Everyone heard what I said, and it hit them like a bomb. "Is she going to report us?" they were obviously thinking. I left it at that. Let them think what they want.

I was feeling angry about what had happened. The church split made me sad, even though I had seen it coming, but particularly because it had all happened three days before my departure. I felt deceived and betrayed because it had happened behind my back. I was also surprised to see how easily the village people had let themselves be influenced.

At the police headquarters in Manna, I went directly to the security office where I always had to report.

"I would like to de-register. Straight after Christmas, I am leaving the village for good." The police officer immediately referred me to the office of his superior, who was happy to see me and to have a chat with me.

"What is the situation in the village? Is everything okay?" he asked.

"Oh, help! What do I say now?" I wondered. "I don't want to tell untruths."

The man noticed my hesitation and kept digging. Hesitantly, I told him about the service of the previous evening, and bit by bit he got the whole story out of me. An hour later, when I was sitting back in my car, I almost felt like a betrayer myself.

"Why did I let myself be questioned like that?" I was incredibly cross with myself and shocked at how easily I, too, had allowed myself to be influenced.

# Chapter 57

# Christmas Visit to Siginim

After the events of the day, I felt very weary when I got back from Manna. But I had to keep my promise and drive to the evening Christmas service in Siginim with the village young people. It would be my goodbye visit too.

It was already getting dusk when I got the car out of the garage again. I couldn't see any of the young people, but suddenly they all appeared. Someone pushed a wooden bench in between the benches already fixed on either side of the cargo area and the young lads sat straddled across it. It was going to be a tight squeeze, so we decided to have the guitar in the front. We prayed before we set off. On the way, I made the young people count how many there were so that I would know how many I needed to take back home at the end of the evening. There were 22 in all! The car was totally overloaded. I drove carefully. Going down the mountain, I noticed that the bottom of the car was scraping the ground. The rain of the previous weeks meant there were deep ruts in the clay soil. "If the axle breaks or the brakes fail and we all end up in the ravine – it does not bear thinking about!" the thought flashed through my mind. The newspaper headlines could read, "Toyota crashes into ravine. White lady driver. 23 fatalities!" No-one would believe it! I prayed and changed back to first gear.

When we reached the outskirts of Manna, there was a knock on the cab window from someone at the back.

"What is the matter?" I asked.

"Just stop a minute so that people can get off the roof. You are not supposed to be sitting on the roof in built up areas."

Ouch! I didn't even know I had passengers on the roof. When everyone was inside, they knocked as a signal for me to drive on. At the end of the town I was not called on to stop. After all, anyone who can climb like a monkey up 20-metre high palm trees can manage to climb onto the roof of a moving car.

The church in Siginim was quite big and there were many guests from nearby congregations. Once again the programme filled the whole evening: the service, speeches, and performances by different groups. Our young people were contributing a singing number. After the service, the principal of the Christian school wanted to talk to me and invited me over to his house. There we were served delicious home-made cookies and traditional food. The teachers of the Christian schools were supported financially by a German organisation and I functioned as a trustee of the organisation. He wanted to know what would happen in the future once I had left. Personally, I was not entirely convinced whether the current management system, under the leadership of Pak Yakardin, would work. As the conversation went on, we broached the subject of the church split, which was also manifest there. It was sad, but we could not find any solutions.

Long after midnight, we started to make our way home. On the way, I kept wanting to fall asleep. To keep awake, I asked the girls in the front cab to tell me funny stories. In that way, we safely reached our village around two o'clock in the morning.

# Chapter 58

# Leaving the Village

On Christmas day, I drove into Manna one more time. In our post office box, I found a whole pile of Christmas mail, including a letter from my mother. She wrote that father had been admitted to hospital, shortly after his birthday at the beginning of December, due to pains in his leg. Further tests were still to come and that, as yet, there was no diagnosis. She said that she was so happy that I would soon be back in Germany.

"I wonder what that means," I mused. "Is this what God was preparing me for two years ago?"

Two years earlier, I had been in Germany for my father's 70th birthday. As I was saying goodbye to friends at the airport, one of them asked me, "Well, how does it feel to say goodbye?" At that moment I had had a feeling that I would not see my father again, or if I did, then under difficult circumstances. That feeling had dogged me for the last two years. When I rang him on his birthday at the beginning of the month, he was fine. There had seemed to be no reason to worry and, after all, I expected to be back in Germany in a few short weeks. Had I got it wrong? What did the letter mean?

"Wati, why might you get pains in your leg?"

She thought for a moment. "It could be thrombosis or it could come from a slipped disc if there was a trapped nerve."

"And how dangerous is something like that?"

"It's hard to say. A thrombosis can lead to death."

That information was not terribly helpful or reassuring. I decided I would phone my mother as soon as I reached Bengkulu.

A leaving service had been planned at church for the evening but the events of the last couple of days with regard to the church split overshadowed my departure. Representatives from both sides came, but there was a palpable tension in the air. The ladies had cooked a meal for everyone. There were a few thank you speeches full of many lovely, if perhaps meaningless, words. I sensed little warmth.

I too looked back over my time in the village and thanked the congregation for their warm welcome, and apologised for any shortcomings and mistakes I may have made as was customary in the culture. I pointed out that a new chapter was beginning for the congregation. The time of foreign missionaries living in their village was over. Presumably, few foreigners would be visiting the village in the future and there would be less access to financial help from abroad. "This is an opportunity for you to take up greater responsibility. I wish you much courage and wisdom from above. The Lord bless you."

After a meal together, everyone shook my hand to say goodbye and to say thank you.

The next day there was still a lot to pack up and load onto the car. Some of my belongings, especially books, I was going to store with some colleagues in Bengkulu and, if necessary, have them sent on to my next post. All day long, ladies kept dropping in to say good bye personally. It was kind of them but it slowed me down a lot. Some of the men helped me to load suitcases, cardboard boxes, bookshelves, and other pieces of luggage onto my car. I was thankful that despite the dark clouds it was staying dry. It was dusk when I finally got on my way.

On the way to Bengkulu my thoughts wandered back. I had enjoyed living in the village. I had felt safe in the village community and had belonged there. It was so sad that, thanks to the problems brought in by certain outsiders, I was leaving with such a bitter aftertaste. I felt empty and burnt out. What had the years of service there been worth? What had I left behind in the village? A quarrelling congregation!

But I didn't have time to grieve. That would have to wait as right then I needed to direct my thoughts forwards. Before flying to Germany, I still had to go over some of the details with the Indonesian Bible Society with regard to the printing of the New Testament, and I also needed to discuss the alternatives for my continued future involvement with the leadership. At that moment, however, my biggest concern was the welfare of my father. I felt it was important to ring my mother from Bengkulu that evening, to find out what was really wrong with him and how critical his situation was.

# Chapter 59

# Going Home

Although I hadn't planned to arrive so late, I was warmly greeted by my colleagues in Bengkulu and we unloaded the car together. Over a good meal, I told them about the events that had taken place in the village over the past few days. I also mentioned the worrying letter from my mother. After we had eaten, I drove to the telephone exchange in town. It was midnight when I entered the lobby. As Germany is six hours behind Indonesian time, it was not a bad time to ring.

I reached my mother at home. "How is father?"

"He has a slipped disc," she explained, "but the consultant is on his Christmas holidays."

"I am going to be on the road a lot up until I fly home in three weeks. You won't be able to reach me, but I will contact you when I can, so that I can keep up with what is happening," I promised her.

Two days later, on the way to our staff conference in East Java, I had a little bit of time at the airport in Jakarta. I looked for a telephone with an international connection. Mother was at home, but as yet there was no news.

"I'm in Jakarta at the airport right now and have everything with me for my trip home. If you want me to come home now, I'll get on the next plane. Then I'll be home tomorrow morning," I offered.

"No, you need to go to your staff conference. It's okay," she assured me.

I phoned again on New Year's Day. Father was going to be operated on at the University Hospital, but still had to wait for a bed there. I hoped it would take a bit longer so that I would still get to see him before he had surgery. I gave my mother the telephone number at the home of colleagues in Bandung where she could reach me after the staff conference was over.

After the conference, I travelled to Batu to say goodbye to some of the IMF staff members there. I briefly informed the Indonesian leader of the situation in the village. By six o'clock it was dark, and it was wet and cold because it had been raining all afternoon. Nevertheless, I took a bus into town in order to phone home again. My mother was in tears.

"I have just come home to make some lunch," she told me. "Father was going to be transferred to the University Hospital today, but this morning he passed blood. The doctors have to get a handle on that first before he can be transferred." The impression I had had at our last goodbye in Germany came back to mind. So, there were complications after all!

The next day, I was sitting on the night bus to Bandung. While the bus was roaring through the darkness, I closed my eyes and tried to sleep. "But why am I sitting on this bus?" the thought struck me. "I should be sitting on a plane to Germany!"

When I arrived at the home of my colleagues in Bandung, I immediately tried to rebook my flight to Frankfurt, but all the flights with my airline were fully booked for the next two weeks. I asked to be put on the waiting list.

"Tonight we are invited to a wedding," my colleague Else told me. "The groom is Pak Nimrod, from the IMF. You know him, don't you?"

"Yes, I do. I used to work quite closely with him in Batu."

"Why don't you come along," she suggested. "I'm sure he would be really pleased." And so I let her persuade me to go along to the wedding. It was a big reception in a hotel. There too, among those guests, I could not help thinking, "Why am I here at this wedding? I should be sitting in a plane to Germany."

The following morning the phone rang at 7 o'clock. It was my sister.

"Father had emergency surgery yesterday. He is in intensive care."

"Thanks for the news. I am trying to get home as quickly as I can."

While I sipped hot coffee, I deliberated with Else. "Today is Sunday," she reminded me. "All the travel agencies are closed but I think GARUDA[38] is open on Sunday mornings from 9 o'clock onwards. Let's get over there as soon as we can."

The GARUDA office was open.

"Do you still have a space on the flight to Frankfurt tonight?"

The lady checked on her computer. "No, sorry, it is fully booked."

"What about tomorrow?"

"That is also fully booked, and so is the day after tomorrow." It seemed hopeless.

"What would a ticket cost?" I asked anyway. She stated the price. It was three times the cost of my original ticket.

"Do you have the telephone numbers of the other large airlines like Lufthansa, KLM, MAS etc.?"

She handed me the phone book and I wrote down the numbers. When I rang them, I mostly got, "We are unable to connect you to this number." I had not even got through. I was frustrated.

---

[38] *GARUDA* is the Indonesian national airline.

193

"There is a 5-star hotel here in Bandung which has a travel agency. I think it is open on Sundays. Let's go there," Else suggested.

The sign on the travel agency door indeed advertised Sunday opening, but everything was dark inside the office and there was no-one there.

"Why don't you go straight to the airport in Jakarta and see how you get on from there," Else said.

Back at home we discussed my options. The next train to Jakarta left in half an hour. That was too tight. "I'll take the one at midday," I decided.

"Do you have enough money for the flight?" Else asked. I emptied my purse. I had some cash, some D-Mark notes, and some dollars in the form of travellers' cheques – no way near enough for a ticket.

"We have some cash, dollars and also D-Marks. You can have it," Else offered.

"I have my BCA[39] account book with me. As far as I am aware, they have a branch at the airport. That should be enough," I replied.

"No, it would be better if you had it on you. Better safe than sorry." I let her persuade me. All I needed to do was to lock my suitcase and then I was ready to go.

I reached the airport in Jakarta at four in the afternoon. The ticket counter wasn't hard to find.

"I need a ticket to Frankfurt for tonight, please." The employee checked on his computer.

"I am very sorry, but there are no spaces." I looked at him, feeling very disappointed and not knowing what to do next.

"Would you be willing to fly via another country?" he asked.

"What do you mean?"

"You know, you could fly from Singapore or Bangkok for example."

"Yes, of course!"

I waited again. "Yes, I can offer you a place on a Singapore Airlines flight leaving just after midnight from Singapore." I was relieved.

"And how much is it?" He gave me the price. It was as much as the GA-RUDA ticket had been going to cost.

"I'll take it. I just have to change money at the bank."

The bank was right next door. I exchanged what I had, but it was not enough. I decided to cash my travellers' cheques. The man behind the counter pointed to a sign. "These are American Express cheques. We don't accept these."

---

[39] BCA stands for Bank Central Asia.

I got out my account book. "Unfortunately, the bank is closed. It is only the Bureau de Change that is open."

I looked at the man, feeling totally confused. I could not believe what was happening: There was a seat on a plane for tonight and it was all going to fail for the sake of 100 dollars because the bank was shut and the money changer wouldn't accept my cheques. "God," I prayed, "what is your solution?"

I went back to the ticket counter and explained my situation to the employee.

"There is another bank here inside the airport. Let me ask if they will exchange American Express cheques."

A little while later he was back. "Yes, they will take American Express. But I have to go with you otherwise they won't let you past the controls. I'll come out to the door."

It was ten to five when I finally held my flight ticket in my hand. "There is a flight to Singapore at a quarter past eight, or you could try to get on the next flight at half past five. The counter is just over there. I wish you a pleasant journey."

I managed to get a seat on the first flight. In Singapore, I had lots of time before my connecting flight and had no problems cashing in my travellers' cheques. I bought a phone card and rang my mother. "I'm in Singapore. My plane lands in Frankfurt at seven o'clock tomorrow morning."

Then I rang the mission headquarters in Germany. The housekeeper answered the phone. "I'm in Singapore on my way to Germany. My phone card is just about to run out. If you want more information, then please ring my mother at home."

I had not been able to buy any souvenirs for my family in Bandung, so I bought a large bouquet of orchids at the airport. It was a long flight and I was worried about my father.

I was picked up in Frankfurt.

"Can we go straight to the hospital?" I asked.

"No. Father is in intensive care and we can only visit at certain times. You won't be allowed to take the flowers."

We were finally allowed to visit him around midday. He was on a ventilating machine and in an induced coma. He was lying totally still in front of me. His rib cage rose and fell in time with the machine. I was shocked. In Indonesia, I had seen several corpses as they were kept at the house before being taken to be buried. But seeing my own father so lifeless in front of me was different. I felt like shouting, "Detach the machines so that he wakes up and I can talk to him." And yet I was thankful that I had been prepared and that I was therefore better able to deal with the situation.

His condition deteriorated from day to day. When the phone rang during breakfast on Saturday morning, I looked at my mother and said, "It is for you."

It was the news of his death.

# Epilogue

# Christmas Songs in Serawai

A good year later, I returned to Indonesia and settled in the city of Beng-kulu where I worked with the church in Curup and helped them to translate God's word into various local languages. Once in a while, I would think back to my time in Napal Melintang with mixed feelings. I had spent many lovely years there and had grown to love the people in that village. But the church split had left a deep scar in my heart. Saina, a daughter of my former neighbour, Mak Ria, was now living with me. She was attending high school in the city and helped me around the house.

For the first time the Serawai Christians from the various churches in Bengkulu wanted to organise a joint Christmas service with each group taking part of the service. The Serawai people from my church wanted to sing a Christmas song out of the Indonesian hymn book. In the afternoon they practised at my house.

"Shouldn't we sing at least one song in Serawai? It is, after all, a Serawai Christmas service," I suggested at our gathering.

"But none of the Serawai songs are Christmas songs," they replied.

We agreed that I would translate a Christmas song. After the others left, I started on it straight away and asked Saina to help me. When we had fin-ished we remained sitting together behind the house.

"Are you satisfied now?" With this question, Saina looked at me expec-tantly.

I hesitated with my answer and thought for a moment.

Finally I replied truthfully, but firmly, "No, I am not satisfied."

"But why not? You've now got your Serawai Christmas song."

"Yes, the words might be Serawai, but it is a translated song with a western melody. It would be better to have something with one of your own tunes. That would be a lot more convincing. You know, like the way you all sometimes sang when we walked, taking turns to sing a line. You could sing Bible texts according to your own melodies."

"Hmm, you are right. Do it then!" she challenged me.

"I might be able to sing along to your tunes, but I can't make up any of my own. That needs to come from you folk. It's in you. You have to do that, Saina. I'll help you."

"No way. I really can't," Saina protested. "But my Uncle Mahar, he is good at that. He often grabs his guitar at home and starts singing Serawai tunes. My aunt doesn't like it though and so he stops. But he is actually really good at it."

Pak Mahar had been pastor at a GEKISIA church in Bengkulu for many years. His wife was Javanese and came from a totally different culture. That same evening I called Pastor Mahar and asked him to come by the next day.

The following morning, he knocked at my door. After a short greeting, I gave him my guitar. "Please, could you play us a Serawai tune?"

He looked at me incredulously. I explained to him what it was about.

"And I thought there was a problem with my niece Saina," he said with relief.

He tuned the guitar to suit his purpose, one of the strings a semitone higher than normal and began to play and sing. I felt excited, but after a while he gave up.

"Sorry, it won't work. I really am not very good at this."

"Why?" I protested. I could see my vision disappearing. "That sounded great!"

"No, that was nothing. I can't do it on my own. I know someone who can play the guitar much better than I can. He should do it."

"Well, bring him along then and you can practice here." I was determined not to give up.

Sure enough, two days later they both came to me in the evening. After introducing ourselves, they began to put a tune to the angels' message from the Christmas story. But they could not really get into it.

"You know," they said, "the Serawai tunes don't really fit with the Christmas story."

"Why ever not?"

"Serawai tunes are usually about sad events or about longings, but the Christmas message is about a happy event. Somehow it doesn't quite work."

"You could take another story," I suggested, "like the one about the lost son. That would work, wouldn't it?"

"Well, I suppose Jesus being born in a stable and lying in a manger would work," Pak Mahar admitted, and they continued practising.

On the evening of the Christmas service, the Methodist church was full of the Serawai Christians and their guests. A large part of the programme was in Indonesian and only the Christmas story was read out of the Serawai New Testament. The second to last item on the programme of events was our translated song. At first some people laughed as it was strange for them to hear Serawai words sung to that particular tune, but then they began to listen attentively.

Finally, Pak Mahar and his friend came forward. A hush descended as the people heard the first sounds from the guitar. This was their music, and it went straight to their hearts. The Serawai Christians were hearing the angel's Christmas message in a way that was uniquely their own. It had become so quiet, you could have heard a pin drop. Everyone was deeply moved by what they were hearing. No one wanted to get up afterwards, all wanting to hold that moment a little longer. For many, especially for the older people, it was the highlight of the evening.

Later on, Sidarni came up to me. She was a Bible school student and was on her way to her village for the Christmas holidays. "Ibu Hildegard, I didn't know it was possible to sing the message of the Bible to our own tunes. This would be a wonderful way to spread the message in the villages."

I was moved by her realisation and prayed that some of the Serawai people would take hold of the opportunity to share the Christian message with their own people in their own peculiar way.

# About WEC International

WEC International (Worldwide Evangelisation for Christ) is a world-wide mission organisation with workers from different countries and denominations. The mission was founded in 1913 by the Englishman C.T. Studd and his wife Priscilla. They started the work in the interior of Africa. From there it spread throughout the world.

With over 1,800 workers in over 80 countries, today WEC is truly an international mission agency. WEC International reaches out to people who have limited or no access to the good news of Jesus Christ, particularly where there is no church. They work in multicultural teams helping worshipping communities of believers multiply among these people.

http://www.wecinternational.org

# About the Author

Hildegard Berg grew up in West Germany giving her life to the Lord as a teenager. During her studies of computer science at the University of Karlsruhe, she was wholeheartedly engaged in the work of the Christian union. After graduation God called her into Bible translation with WEC International in Indonesia. In 1981 she travelled to Indonesia for the first time, learning the language and culture in Batu, East Java.

From 1984 to 1992 she lived in NapalMelintang, a small village in South Sumatra without running water or electricity. She learned the local language, Serawai, from the village people, reduced it to writing and translated the New Testament for the local Christian church.

Later, she was engaged in various ministries in Bengkulu and Malang, East Java. Following the Independence of East Timor, she moved to its capital Dili in 2000.

Since her return to Germany in 2003, she works in the finance office of the WEC sending base in Eppstein. In 2009 she married Henning Herrmann, the former sending base leader.

# Europe:
# Restoring Hope

## Deborah Meroff

The continent known for over 1000 years as the heartland of Christianity has gone into spiritual arrest. Drawing from the experience of many individuals and organisations, this book takes a hard look at four population groups at the centre of Europe's heart trouble: marginalised people, Muslims, youth and nominal and secular Europeans. Here is proof that it is possible to restore hope to this great continent when God's people work together. This practical resource supplies all the motivation and information we need to get started.

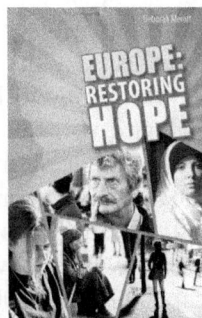

"Europe is very likely a battleground for the future of global Christianity... I hope that whoever reads these pages will be encouraged and inspired to prayer and action."

Jiří Unger
President of the European Evangelical Alliance

"My wife Drena and I have now been based in Europe for 50 years. Debbie Meroff's book True Grit was one of the most important books in our lives, and her new book on Europe is another cutting edge, must-read!"

George Verwer
Founder and International Co-ordinator Emeritus, OM International

"This book shows that God is still at work in Europe. He is building his church despite many challenges. And he wants to see each one of us playing an active part in restoring hope to Europe!"

Frank Hinkelmann
European Director, OM International

ISBN 978-3-941750-06-7
296 pp. · Pb. · £ 14.95 / $ 24.95

VTR Publications
info@vtr-online.com
http://www.vtr-online.com

www.ingramcontent.com/pod-product-compliance
Lightning Source LLC
LaVergne TN
LVHW051627080426
835511LV00016B/2225